# The Fourth Man In The Car

Keith Menshouse

WESTBOW
PRESS
A DIVISION OF THOMAS NELSON

Scripture quotations marked "MSG" are taken from the THE MESSAGE. Copyright © by Eugene H. Peterson 1993, 1994, 1995, 1996, 2000, 2001, 2002. Used by permission of NavPress Publishing Group.

Scripture quotations marked "NCV" are taken from the New Century Version. Copyright © 1987, 1988, 1991 by Word Publishing, a division of Thomas Nelson, Inc. Used by permission. All rights reserved.

Scripture quotations marked "NKJV" are taken from the New King James Version. Copyright © 1982 by Thomas Nelson, Inc. Used by permission. All rights reserved.

Scripture quotations marked "NLT" are taken from the Holy Bible, New Living Translation, copyright © 1996. Used by permission of Tyndale House Publishers, Inc., Wheaton, IL 60189 USA. All rights reserved.

WestBow Press books may be ordered through booksellers or by contacting:

WestBow Press
A Division of Thomas Nelson
1663 Liberty Drive
Bloomington, IN 47403
www.westbowpress.com
1-(866) 928-1240

ISBN: 978-1-4497-3083-3 (sc)
ISBN: 978-1-4497-3084-0 (hc)
ISBN: 978-1-4497-3082-6 (e)
Library of Congress Control Number: 2011919857
Printed in the United States of America

WestBow Press rev. date:11/07/2011

To the Fourth Man In The Car on that rainy night of May 7th, 2005 in Catlettsburg, Kentucky. And to the men and women who risked their lives, used their God-given skills and gave of themselves so unselfishly in our greatest time of need. We are eternally grateful.

A special thanks to our dear friend Vincent Naseem, who lovingly painted the artwork used for the cover of this book and who wrote many letters of encouragement to our family.

# Contents

# Forward

I'll never forget the evening of May 7th, 2005. That was the night God finally got my attention.

At the time, I'd been a Christian for about 27 years, and had experienced a number of highs and lows in my walk with Christ. 2005 was a low point. On the outside, I looked like I had it all together spiritually. I was a full-time youth minister and a worship leader. But on the inside, I was disillusioned, discouraged, and wrestling with God.

I had met the Menshouses five years earlier while interviewing for a position at the church Keith pastored. Keith soon became not only my pastor, but my friend as well, and over the next few years, he and his wife, Debbie, would be a constant encouragement to me. Their son, Clark, also became a big part of my life. Not only was Clark a member of my youth group, but from 2004 to 2005, he was the drummer for our church's praise team, which I led. The four of us would often meet up for lunch on Sundays after church, and as May 8th 2005 was Mother's Day, and I was away from home, I had planned on celebrating with the Menshouses. But on Saturday evening, not long after wondering where we'd be eating the next day, my phone rang. That call would be the catalyst God used to change my life forever.

But for me, the story you're about to read actually started two days earlier, on Thursday, May 5th. Keith was scheduled to leave town after lunch on Mother's Day, and I was supposed to preach for him at the evening service. Being a bit of a procrastinator, and unable to decide what to preach, I had planned to use Saturday afternoon to pick my topic and Saturday night to prepare it. On Thursday, I had intended to work on my yard, not my message.

I had just fired up my lawn mower when God spoke to me. Not audibly. But verbally. And clearly.

I stopped the mower, took off my headphones, and stood in absolute silence for a moment. Had I imagined it? Directly hearing the voice of God was not a daily occurrence for me; it didn't even fit with my theology. Had God really just spoken to me? What I had heard was unmistakable: I wasn't supposed to wait until Saturday to pick and prepare my message; I was to prepare my message that night.

I knew what I heard, but I wasn't convinced yet that it was from God. Hesitantly, I asked God to repeat Himself. And the Spirit did repeat Himself. Confused, and a little scared, I said, "O.k., I'll do it tonight." God didn't have my full attention yet, but He'd given me a firm tap on the shoulder.

The mower kicked back on, but I left the headphones off. I suddenly had to decide what I was going to preach. It wasn't an easy decision, because truthfully, I was hoping it would be my last sermon – or at least the last I'd have to preach for a very long time. Just a few weeks earlier I had told Keith, and our church's personnel committee, that I was planning on resigning as youth pastor and worship leader at the end of May. My plan was to go back to school and finish my Master's, but really, school was just an excuse to get out. I was praying and hoping that my pastoring days were over. Ministry can be a grind, and I was being crushed by the weight of my own failed expectations. For too long I'd been so focused on my own calling and my own gifting that I'd lost sight of the One who had called and gifted me.

Of course, I didn't know at the time why God had tapped me on the shoulder that Thursday, why He had so clearly commanded me to prepare my sermon earlier than I had wanted. I had no clue that I would be spending Saturday evening, into the early hours of Sunday morning, in a hospital waiting room, or that I would only have time to grab a handful of hours of sleep before taking Keith's place behind the pulpit that Sunday morning. I could never have predicted how quickly my ministry – my entire life's trajectory – would change, or that the very people who had encouraged and prayed for me would suddenly find themselves in desperate need of my prayers and encouragement.

More than that, I couldn't imagine how much –and how quickly – God would change my heart in the months that followed, as my focus shifted from myself to Christ. But I'll save that story for my own book, if I ever write it. Suffice it to say that I had a front row seat to the testimony which you're about to read. And as I witnessed first-hand the power of God and the effectiveness of prayer, I also discovered what the Apostle Peter meant when he wrote these words in 1Peter 1:7 (ESV): "... that the tested genuineness of your faith – more precious than gold that perishes though it is tested by fire – may be found to result in praise and glory and honor at the revelation of Jesus Christ."

Every now and then, I need the reminder that God gave to Sarah in Genesis18:14 (ESV), when He told the 90 yr. old woman who about to have a son: "Is anything too hard for the LORD?" My memories of these events serve as that reminder.

By the way, you might be wondering what message God had told me to prepare that Thursday while I was cutting grass, the one God wanted my church – and myself – to hear on the morning of May 8th. It was "Hebrews 11: Walking by Faith."

My prayer is that your faith will be rekindled – or ignited for the first time – as you read this story.

DJ Ritchey
Assistant Pastor, Pennwood Bible Church
September, 2011

# Preface
## Do You Believe In Miracles?

*Miracle - pronunciation: 'mir-i-k&l - 1: an extraordinary event manifesting divine intervention in human affairs; 2 : an extremely outstanding or unusual event, thing, or accomplishment. "miracle." Merriam-Webster Online Dictionary. 2006. http://www.merriam-webster.com (1 Jan. 2006).*

In the closing seconds of the 1980 Olympic hockey game between the USA and the Soviet Union, Al Michaels of ABC Sports asked the now famous question, "Do you believe in miracles?" Well, do you? "Sure", you quickly respond ( almost out of some sense of guilt that to hesitate or say otherwise would be sacrilege). I mean miracles happen around us all the time. Don't they?

Every time the sun comes up − every time a child is born − every time someone places their faith in Christ and is born into the family of God. It's a miracle! It's what I like to call a Webster2 miracle. It's "an extremely outstanding or unusual event, thing, or accomplishment", as the *Merriam-Webster Online Dictionary* declares a second meaning of the word. Our normal usage of the word "miracle" means that we are impressed or even in awe of how something was accomplished.

For instance, the beauty of the early morning sunrise, with all of its beautiful shades of color, never ceases to take your breath away. We marvel at the precise timing and dependability of the sun's path and measure our very lives by it. But at the same time we have some measure of comprehension of the "how" and "why" of the sunrise. Remember those junior high science classes on the solar system? Don't you recall the experiments with prisms and the light spectrum? ROY G. BIV? In fact, we not only understand the sunrise – we expect it! So much in fact, that most of the time, we jump out of bed and never give it a second thought.

The same is true for the baby thing. You know, the birds and the bees…junior high health class (we sure learned a lot in junior high). We know where babies come from but we can't keep from staring through the nursery window of the hospital with mouth open in awe and wonder at ten little fingers and ten little toes. It's a miracle! One that you look forward to and expect to happen. You even get a little pressure from the prospective grandparents to make it happen soon (or again).

People even walk into church with the same expectations that the miraculous will happen within the normal frame of reference. There will be worship and the proclamation of the Gospel, and the expectation is that someone will respond to the message and experience the miracle of salvation. I have been a pastor for nearly 25 years and I have seen it hundreds of times. I've watched as God has taken shattered and stained lives and transformed them into lives of hope and forgiveness. Every time it happens I am in awe of the power of God to make such a change in a person's life. At the same time I have also spent those years studying and then teaching about "how" and "why" God performs such a miracle. The Bible is full of teachings and insights that give us an understanding on what is happening - even a commission to proclaim the message so that it will happen to more and more people!

I am truly thankful for Webster2 miracles. But let me ask you, have you ever experienced a Webster1? I had heard others tell about them and I believed that they happened but I had never seen it myself. What's a Webster1 miracle? If we return to the

*Merriam-Webster Online Dictionary* and read the first entry, we will see these words: "an extraordinary event manifesting divine intervention in human affairs".

I remember seeing an interview once with one of the stars of the TV series *Touched By An Angel*. Della Reese played the role of Tess, an angel sent to do God's bidding, in the weekly drama. When asked what she attributed to the show's huge success, she answered, "It's a God thing!" That's exactly what a Webster1 is – a God thing. It's an event that has no explanation – it can't be read in a textbook or seen under the microscope. It can't be expected or anticipated. God just brings it to happen before our very eyes. He intervenes in our human affairs and sets aside the calculating laws of science and the record of history. God does what only God can do in the way that God chooses to do it. Experiencing it doesn't leave a warm, fuzzy feeling. Instead it leaves us speechless and bowed down in reverential fear and trembling at God's awesome power – and His love. This book is the story of a Webster1.

# How Long?

*"But you do not know what will happen tomorrow! Your life is like a mist. You can see it for a short time, but then it goes away."*
James 4:14 (NCV)

How long does it take? One heartbeat? One blink of the eye? One breath? How long does it take for your life to completely change its direction? How quickly can an event challenge everything you thought you knew about life and faith? For our family, it took only one ring of a cell phone.

On the Saturday evening before Mother's Day, 2005, my wife, Debbie, and I were sitting at home in our small third bedroom that had been converted into a family room. It was barely big enough for a recliner, a chair, and a small TV. On this night, however, we had added an ironing board to the mix, because it was Saturday night at the pastor's house! Debbie was getting all the wrinkles out of our Sunday clothes while I was attempting to do the same with the sermon for the next day.

Our sixteen-year-old son, Clark, had followed his normal Saturday night ritual and went to the mall with some friends. They usually spent a couple of hours playing video games and then would grab something to eat before his nine-thirty curfew. While I realize that many parents are afraid to even mention the word "curfew" to their children, we never had a problem with

1

Clark. Maybe that's because we really gave him no option. When he started to drive at sixteen, we simply came to a "meeting of the minds," you might say. We informed him that if we didn't "meet" him at the front door at the agreed upon time, then our "minds" were made up to take his car keys away. Amazingly, he was never late.

It was nearing the curfew time on that Saturday evening and I was changing one of my PowerPoint slides while keeping an eye on a baseball game. I expected to hear the rattle of keys in the door at any second. In fact, Debbie had just asked me if it was about time for Clark to come home and I sort of scolded her and told her not to worry so much. She should relax and trust him more because he always kept his curfew. Then my cell phone rang.

Looking back on it now, five years later, I can't help but be drawn to that ring. I can still hear it in my mind. It's as if the phone was ringing to make an announcement to us—that our lives were about to change forever. In reality it was ringing to announce that our lives had already changed and they would never be the same again. It had already happened.

As I picked up my phone and looked at the display, I smiled and prepared for some good news. The call was coming from Chris, a good friend and member of the church where I served as pastor. Chris and I had been working together on a remodeling project at the church; I assumed he was calling to fill me in on the day's progress report. But not this time. In addition to being a church member and a friend, Chris was a fireman. He worked for our city fire department—a job that we had prayed he would be offered just months before.

As I answered the phone, I heard my fireman friend say to me, "Brother Keith, this is Chris. Clark has been in an accident and it's pretty serious. They're trying to get him out of the car right now. I think you and Debbie should get here as fast as you can." When I heard those words, I knew exactly what they meant.

Chris was trying to tell us that we only had a few minutes to be with Clark before he died.

As I started to ask questions about where the accident was and how badly Clark was injured, I could see the panic growing in Debbie's eyes. Her worst nightmare was coming true in that instant. I felt so helpless because there was nothing I could do to keep it from happening.

I know that the injury or death of a child could be described as any parent's worst nightmare, but it was different for us. We both were nineteen and attending college when we married. I was already preparing to follow God's calling to be a pastor and she was in nursing school. She will tell you that she chose nursing for one reason and one reason only—to make sure that we wouldn't have to struggle all our lives on a pastor's salary. So, needless to say, she has never experienced deep fulfillment from her vocation as a nurse.

The exception to that, however, would be the three years she spent as a nurse in the emergency department and the five years she worked as a flight nurse. I remember how thrilled she was the day she was hired as a flight nurse. The job fit her God-given abilities perfectly.

She's intelligent, loves challenges, and has a keen ability to size up a situations and people in an instant. She's also not afraid to try anything! She was pregnant with Clark while working as a flight nurse in Dayton, Ohio, so she kept a daily log for him about where he had traveled in the helicopter.

But while being a flight nurse might seem glamorous and exciting on the outside, it soon begins to take its toll on the inside. If you've ever watched the television show *ER*, then you know what I mean. Every day she would come home and need to "debrief" about what life-threatening emergencies she had flown into that day. Some might be critical heart patients or neo-natal transports, but most were trauma. Many of them, especially the fatalities, were car wrecks. And most were car wrecks involving teenagers.

For years she had dreaded Clark turning sixteen and beginning to drive. We had talked about it a hundred times and every time I reassured her that she had nothing to worry about. I told her that for starters, she needed to remember that she only saw the worst of the worst and that the odds of that ever being her son were slim to none. Secondly, I reminded her that our son was one of the most timid and careful kids we had ever seen. We actually had to sell a dirt bike that we bought him as a Christmas present when he was younger because he didn't like to ride it. She had nothing to worry about.

Now here we were on this fateful Saturday night and I had just told her again not to worry about him—that he would be home any minute. As I ended the call I started to realize not only that I could not take away her fear, but also that I had lied to her all those years. Her nightmare was about to come true. He wasn't coming home. He wasn't fine. Her baby boy, our only child, was trapped in his car on the side of the road and he was going to die.

# The First Time I Cried

*"In my distress I cried unto the LORD, and he heard me."*
*Psalm 120:1 (NKJV)*

When I ended the call, I was expecting Debbie to slump to the floor and start crying hysterically. Nobody could love their kid more than she loved Clark. How would I get her to him? Would I have to call 911 to get emergency help for her?

But in that moment of our greatest need, God did something in her that I'll never fully understand. He flipped on the flight nurse switch that had been off since shortly after Clark was born. She didn't panic or hesitate for one second. She didn't even shed a tear. Instead she just gave me a firm, confident command: "Let's go! Take me to him!"

In seconds we were in the car and headed for the accident scene. It took us about five minutes to get there, most of which we spent in silence. Debbie said only one thing to me on the way there: "Hurry, but be careful." I knew that those were words coming from the nurse who had ridden in dozens of ambulances to get to places the helicopter could not land safely.

As we rounded a curve and started up a hill, we could see emergency lights in the distance. As we got closer it seemed that there were ambulances, fire trucks, and police cars everywhere. Traffic was stopped and pulled off to the side of the road about two hundred yards from the scene, so we parked the car and started out on foot. There was still no panic - not in her voice, not even in her steps as we got closer to the sight we will never forget.

Shortly before Clark turned sixteen, we began looking for a car for him to drive. He never asked for one and certainly didn't voice any preferences about one, so his mom picked one out for him. She had some thoughts on the subject, even if he didn't. She wanted a car that was safe, dependable, and would be easily visible to other drivers.

One night while she and I were out shopping, we came across what we thought would be the perfect car. It was a four-cylinder, standard-shift Mitsubishi Lancer. Our theory was that it would be easy on gas, easy to drive, and easy to see because it was a color called "lightning yellow." It nearly glowed in the dark. To top things off, we put a green fluorescent light around his license plate that would flash when he applied his brakes. We drove it home to Clark, sight unseen, and he loved it. Everybody was happy.

But now as we reached the top of the hill, we could see his bright yellow Lancer completely wrapped around a utility pole exactly at the driver's door. The car had hit the pole with such a force that it snapped the pole in two and the pole had fallen onto the roof of the car. The metal of the rear and front fenders were only inches apart on the other side of the pole. The car literally looked like it had been cut into two pieces. The utility pole was now inside the car where the driver's seat had been. The passenger seat had been completely broken off its bolts and debris was everywhere.

My first thought when I saw the car was, "There's no chance he's alive." Just as that thought passed through my mind, Chris came running up to us and took Debbie by the hand to guide her to the car. Just getting to the car was extremely dangerous because of fallen electrical lines that were still live. Sparks lit up the silhouette of the car along with dozens of emergency lights.

As we finally got across the roadside ditch and up to the car, we could see Clark still in the vehicle. A flight nurse – yes a flight nurse – was reaching through the rear window in an attempt to supply oxygen to him through a tube he had skillfully managed to insert through Clark's nose and into his lungs. Teams of firefighters continued to saw away at the car trying to get him free. His legs were pinned in the console of the car and they couldn't get him out. Blood was everywhere.

My immediate reaction was one of numbness and helplessness. I stood a few feet from the car and looked on at my son lying unconscious and outstretched in what was left of the interior of the car.

Debbie's reaction was completely different. She ran right up to the backseat driver's side window and leaned through. Clark's head was only a foot or so from that opening and she grabbed his hand and immediately began yelling to him, "You hang in there Clark. You fight buddy. It's Momma, Clark - you fight!" I often joke that she scared him to life with that speech. It's what she had done for hundreds of people over the years as she worked to save their lives.

It seemed that just as soon as she had gotten those words out that Chris approached us and told us we needed to leave immediately for the hospital. Clark would be flown to a regional trauma center and Chris wanted us to be at the hospital when the chopper landed.

I later found out that there were two other reasons that we were instructed to leave quickly. First was the expectation that they would lose him soon. He had been trapped in the car for over an hour and for severe trauma cases they refer to that time as the "golden hour". His time had run out. Secondly, they still could not get his legs freed. They had been cutting away at the car for over an hour with no results. They were going to try one final plan - pull the car apart with two fire trucks. If it failed, then they would need to amputate his legs in order to get him out of the car. I'm glad we weren't aware of either scenario at that moment.

The thought of leaving Clark in the car was almost too much for Debbie to handle. Part of the problem was she wanted to make sure he was receiving the right kind of treatment at the scene — the kind she would have given. But the other part was a mother didn't want to leave her son hurting and alone.

When we walked up to the scene I had noticed a lady standing very close to the car. I assumed she was with one of the volunteer fire departments but she actually lived in the house just above where the accident happened. Her name was Missy. Missy watched Debbie struggle with whether to go or stay for a few seconds and then she stepped in, wrapped her arms around Debbie and asked, "Are you his mother?" When Debbie nodded, Missy said, "You go to the hospital. I promise you I will stay here and hold his hand for you. I won't leave him." At that moment she gave us an immeasurable gift — the security that we needed to take the next step.

The emergency crews helped us back down to our car and I started on the 30 minute drive to the hospital where Clark would arrive. As we pulled away from the scene, Debbie instructed me to take her to the landing zone that had been temporarily set up for the HealthNet chopper about a half-mile from the accident. I remember thinking that stopping there wouldn't be such a good idea. It would cost us time and there was nothing we could do there. But she was still in flight nurse mode and I took it more as a demand than a request.

As we pulled into the parking lot where the helicopter was stationed, she started out of the car before I could even get it stopped. There would be many points over the next year where my heart broke for the pain that Debbie was in but perhaps none more than this moment. She ran over to the pilot, who had this bewildered look on his face, and she started to tell him who she was. She told him that she had been a flight nurse and that her son was on the way to him. And then she begged him to take good care of her son and get him there safely. She made him promise her that they would take good care of her only child.

The pilot graciously gave her a hug and assured her that the entire crew would do their best. We got back into the car not knowing what tremendous pressure was already on the shoulders of the pilot that night. No more than thirty minutes before the wreck occurred, a band of showers had started to enter the area. The hospital serving as the regional trauma center that night was situated in the mountains of Huntington, West Virginia – at least a thirty minute drive from the accident scene. Rain in the mountains means extremely low cloud cover. It's the one condition that grounds a flight program the quickest. Miraculously – and I don't use that word lightly – the crew was able to take the transport before being grounded. If the call had come an hour later, then they would not have been able to fly that night. Now, at just past 10 PM, this understanding pilot was not only shouldering our burden for Clark but also the burden of returning his crew safely to the trauma center in worsening conditions.

When Debbie got back in the car it was as if she felt her "job" was done. She slowly stopped being a flight nurse and started being a mother again. As we rushed down the interstate towards the hospital, the emotions and the tears that we were both holding back started to just pour out. I really don't know how we made it safely to the hospital. To say we cried on the way would be the world's greatest understatement.

Up to this point I had experienced fear, sorrow, panic and a range of other emotions. But on the way to that hospital, I experienced something I had never felt in my entire life – hopelessness. In my heart it was as though Clark had already died. It was then and only then that I knew what the Psalmist meant when he said, "I cried unto the Lord."

I suppose that when I had read in the Bible of people crying out to God that I took it to mean that they were either trying to get his attention or were crying on his shoulder. I imagined a prayer saying either, "Hey God! I'm having a problem here!" or "God this really hurts and I need somebody to talk to." I had prayed that way before. But this was different. For the first time I was begging God for something – and I mean begging. I wasn't bargaining with him or making promises. And it wasn't that I felt I needed to beg for something he didn't want to give me or that I had to change his mind. I was honestly pouring my heart out to him because I knew that my Lord was Clark's only hope to live. We had been to the scene. We both knew that there was no chance for our son to survive.

So from somewhere inside me that I had never been aware of, came a desperate cry for God's help. But would he hear me?

# A Familiar Sound

*"I knew you before I formed you in your mother's womb.*
*Before you were born I set you apart"*
*Jeremiah 1:5 (NLT)*

It was after 11PM when we pulled into the Emergency Department parking lot. As we got out of the car we could see some familiar faces. Ten to fifteen friends from our church had already heard the news and were there to give us some much needed hugs and encouragement. The HealthNet chopper, however, was not there.

We quickly got inside and identified ourselves to the medical staff. They were tremendous. They escorted us to a private waiting area and told us that Clark was in the air and should arrive within the next ten minutes. That would have been great news to both of us except it had now been over two hours since the accident happened. Since the "golden hour" had come and gone twice, we both knew that it would take a miracle for him to be unloaded alive and now almost a certainty that extensive brain damage would have occurred due to swelling of the brain and lack of oxygen.

Every second seemed like another hour to me, so I decided to wait in sight of the helipad to see them land. Debbie just couldn't do it. She told me to go outside and she would wait inside with the others. So I walked outside that Emergency Department and stood alone about a hundred feet from an empty landing zone.

I stared up at a black sky and listened for what used to be a welcome sound. When Clark was just a toddler, we sometimes took Debbie to work. If her shift was going to end with the flight crew returning empty from a transport, then Momma - as Clark always called Debbie - would call us just before they left to return to home base. Clark and I would go to the helipad at the hospital where she worked and wait for her to land. I would tease him every few seconds and say, "Do you hear Momma coming?" He would giggle and shake his head. When she did finally get near, it was an unmistakable sound. As the sound of the arriving chopper got louder and louder, he would get more and more excited. Momma would land and when all was clear, the pilot would take him out and let him see the chopper. How's that for a grand entrance?

Now over a decade later, I find myself looking up at the sky waiting to hear that familiar sound. Part of me wants to jump up and down when I hear the sound of the rotor blades and part of me wants to cover my ears and run away. Will they unload my son somehow still fighting for his life or will they unload a body draped in a white sheet? Either way, I knew I had to stand there and wait - and watch.

When we arrived they had given us an estimated arrival time of ten minutes but now we were at fifteen and I still heard nothing. I must have looked down at my watch about a dozen times until finally I heard the sound of the helicopter in the distance. Slowly it made its way to the pad and landed. I had watched this dozens of times and I knew that they would have to go through a shutdown procedure in order for it to be safe for the crew to unload the patient.

As I stretched over the railing to get a glimpse of what the crew was doing, the door finally swung open and one flight nurse emerged. She was quickly joined by some help from the ground crew and all I could see was a crowd around the cargo door. The gurney unloads from the chopper and now the wheels extend. I still can't see through the crowd that is gathering around the flight crew. Then they start to push the gurney towards the Emergency Department door and they are moving quickly. Finally I see Clark's head strapped to the board and they are still working on him – he is still alive! How could that be? It's been almost two and a half hours since the wreck and he is still alive.

I ran inside to give the news to Debbie and we cried together just thankful that he had made it this far. We had no idea what would be ahead but God had answered our prayers for this part of the journey. Clark was now just fifty feet from us, receiving the best medical care possible.

Someone came in from the hospital to give us the official word that Clark was now in the ER and they would let us back to see him as soon as possible. In the meantime, they wanted to ask me to take care of his admission paperwork just outside the waiting room. The hospital staff had been so kind not to push anything on us while we waited for him to arrive, so I was willing to follow the staff back to the main ER waiting area.

As I rounded the corner into view of the waiting room, I couldn't believe what I saw. Dozens of people had now filled the room in support of our family and to pray for Clark. There were staff members and deacons and friends from our church. There were friends Clark had made at the local mall's video arcade and kids from his high school. There were pastors from other churches and people that I had never met all sitting in small groups with tears filling their eyes. I asked the hospital representative if I could see them for a second and nearly one hundred people gathered around me as I gave them what little news we had at that moment. All I could tell them was that he was alive and that their prayers were much needed – not only that night but through whatever the next few days and weeks might bring. Many of them stayed there halfway into the night.

As I went over to start on the paperwork, though, I remember thinking something was odd about such a crowd. I could understand the large number from our church because people naturally want to reach out to help the pastor's family when they go through tragedy. I had been there for them many times and now they wanted to be there for us. But what seemed odd was the number of kids from the high school.

Clark had always been a great student who was liked by his peers but his personality was pretty quiet –even shy. He was certainly not "Mr. Popularity" and because of his love for computers he tended to hang out with the "gamers", but now the room was filled with athletes and cheerleaders and other kids that I had never seen him with. It seemed odd.

The hospital staff quickly got the paperwork taken care of so I could return to the private waiting room. As soon as I got back, I noticed a change in Debbie. She was like a caged tiger, walking back and forth in the small room. She had definitely returned to flight nurse mode. Her eyes were fixed on the door and I knew her mind was racing through hundreds of scenarios she had managed from the other side of that door. She was like a supercomputer needing data to be input – what were his vital signs? How were they managing his airway? What procedures had they performed in flight?

I looked at her and before I could even ask what was wrong she said, "I want to see him." And then she added firmly, "Now!" The hospital had provided a chaplain to help with the flow of information, so the chaplain invited us to go with her to visit the nurse's station and find out when we could see Clark.

On the way to the station, Debbie quickly figured out which treatment room he was in and headed for the curtain! The nurse at the station told us that we couldn't go in yet because he was still being evaluated. Just as Debbie was about to enter the room, the trauma surgeon stepped into the hallway and rather forcefully informed us that we could not enter. Clark was being prepared to transport for a CT Scan and we would have to wait until he returned from the test.

What the surgeon didn't know was that "forcefully" is not the way to communicate with my wife. It ignites a fuse within her that's going to create an explosion. As I held my arm around my wife, I could immediately feel every muscle in her body stiffen. Her lower jaw jutted slightly forward and her stare locked on the doctor like the radar system of a heat-seeking missile. She took a step forward towards the curtain.

I knew a battle was getting ready to ensue and my money was on Debbie! As the doctor started to turn to go back into the room, Debbie yelled out (and I do mean yelled), "I know my rights as a parent of this patient and I WILL see him right now!" Without any argument the doctor pulled back the curtain and told us that we should be prepared for what we were going to see. Almost as a "Thank you", Debbie said very quietly, "I promise we won't get in your way."

I cannot describe what a relief it was just to see him for that short time in the ER. I realize the hospital had our best interests in mind. Most parents would have been shocked to see their sixteen year-old in Clark's condition. But for us it was a comfort. Debbie had worked rooms and cases like this for years and I had stood beside and prayed with critical patients hundreds of times in my ministry. This was nothing new to either of us.

Leaving him near death in his car just an hour earlier was a weight we no longer could bear. Now just seeing him again brought some relief. He was on a ventilator, had two chest tubes inserted and there were numerous IVs running but his heart was still beating. Just to see that gave me hope again. The short time in the room was Debbie's chance to immediately evaluate how he was being treated and assess for herself what condition he was really in.

The nurses finished connecting a few lines and then stepped out for just a second. We took those few seconds to pray for and with Clark. I leaned down to his ear and again asked God to bring him through this. I asked God to give him comfort from any pain he was having and to let Clark know that he was with him. In just a few seconds the curtain was pulled back and they were ready to take him for his first of many CT scans and x-rays. We walked alongside to the elevator and then kissed him goodbye and returned to the waiting room.

Of course everyone wanted to know "How is he doing?" and "What did they say?", but we didn't have any answers to give them. Most of our friends and family couldn't begin to picture what we had just seen, even if we tried to describe it. All we could tell them was that Clark had been taken for some initial tests and that they promised to give us an update soon. So for now, all we could do was wait.

# One Decision

*"The Lord directs the steps of the godly. He delights in every detail of their lives. Though they stumble, they will never fall, for the Lord holds them by the hand."Psalm 37:23-24 (NLT)*

It took about almost another hour for the tests to be completed on Clark. Some of the people in the general waiting room had gone home, at least with the knowledge that Clark was still alive. Our "inner circle" of people in the private waiting room was still with us and we had managed at that point to at least begin some conversation that was intended to get our minds off of waiting.

Around 1AM there was a tap on the door and the chaplain quietly stepped into the room. She said the doctor wanted to give us a report and asked again if we were his parents, which was a polite way to ask everyone else to exit the room. We reassured her that all of the family and friends who were present were welcome to hear what the doctor had to say. As she stepped back, the same trauma surgeon that had caused such a reaction from Debbie stepped into the room. This time, however, we could sense compassion about what we were going through and apologies were quickly given and accepted on both sides.

As the doctor began to describe the initial assessment of Clark's injuries we were encouraged and yet hopelessly discouraged. On the positive side he had sustained no damage to his internal organs, his limbs were intact and thanks to the work of the emergency crews and flight nurses, he had received oxygen from the first few moments after the impact.

In fact, we later learned that the accident happened in front of the home of a retired paramedic named Bill. He was home that night when he heard the crash and then suddenly lost all power to his home. He immediately grabbed his kit, which he still kept ready at home, and rushed to find out what had happened. Isn't it just like God to prepare someone for a lifetime to be there for you when you need them the most? As Bill came up to the car window, he could see Clark's body lying across the interior. He was familiar with the sound he was hearing – the sound of someone gasping for breath as their airway began to fill with blood. He had saved untold numbers of lives over his years of service and now our Heavenly Father had him in place to use his skills on our son. At great risk to his own personal safety, Bill leaned into the car to keep Clark's airway open until the paramedics arrived to intubate.

On the negative side, Clark had broken his femur and had several fractures to his hands and wrists. None of those injuries were life-threatening. But the doctor finally came to the worst of the news – he had sustained massive head trauma which, we later found out, caused a skull fracture from his left temple all the way around the back of his skull to his right ear canal.

Debbie and I were thinking the same thing at that moment but she voiced it first. "Tell us the truth" she said, "Don't hold anything back. How bad is it?" The doctor gathered her thoughts for a second and said, "It's the worst head bleed I've ever seen on a CT scan."

We sat in stunned silence, regretting we had asked for such honesty. She went on to tell us that at the moment he was stabilized but things could change at any moment because pressure was building on the brain from the bleeding and swelling. The next hour would be the most critical. As she continued with the honesty we had requested, she let us know that if he did live through the night that there would be almost no chance of a normal life after such massive head trauma.

The doctor said that he would be transferred to the Pediatric Intensive Care Unit or the "PICU" as we came to know it. As she left the room I remember looking around at the faces of our family and friends who were with us. Some of them had started to cry and others were just staring blankly at the wall. I could tell from their expressions that I had heard the doctor correctly. She didn't believe Clark would make it through the night and if he did live then he would be seriously disabled and probably institutionalized.

Debbie leaned over on my shoulder and we held each other for a while. After a few minutes she said softly to me, "I don't care what he's like or what we have to do to take care of him, I just want by baby boy to live." I think that was a moment of promise for both of us. We were promising each other, promising Clark and promising God that if he chose to miraculously spare Clark's life we would do whatever it took to care for him the rest of our lives. It was now crystal clear - if Clark was going to live it would take a miracle from God.

After sitting together for a few more minutes, I thought about all the others who were still outside in the main waiting area. They had been waiting and praying for several hours and they needed to be updated too. So I went down the hallway and gathered the remaining people around me and told them what we knew at that moment. I thanked them for coming to be with us but assured them they could not do anything else for us that night. It would be days before Clark could have any visitors.

As they started to file out of the room, many of them stopped to give me a hug and promise that their church would pray for Clark the next day during their church's Sunday service. I fully believe those prayers made a difference. There were dozens of churches and hundreds of believers praying the next morning during Clark's most critical hours. God honors and answers prayer.

Among the last to leave were the kids from Clark's high school and from our church's youth group. Some of the school kids I knew pretty well because they had been to our house to play video games with Clark. Others were complete strangers to me. It still puzzled me as to why they were there but it just wasn't high on my priority list to figure it out.

The final ones, which I almost had to threaten to get them to leave, were a few of Clark's closest friends from our church. They were like family to us. They were usually at our house several times a week and Clark played in a praise band with a couple of them. They obviously didn't want to leave, so I sat down with them for a second mostly to see how they were handling it. They had some questions for me about how Clark really was and I told them what the doctor had told us.

As we sat there for a moment, I realized I had a question they might be able to help me with. It's the question that was the most obvious but I hadn't had time to think clearly enough to ask it. So I asked, "Do any of you know what happened tonight?"

I had already started to put some theories together in my own mind about what had happened that night. One contributing factor was probably the weather. It had started to rain a little before 9PM and the accident happened just after that. With his inexperience driving on slick roads, I thought that certainly played a part. It was also evident that what I saw at the crash site had to be the result of tremendous force and that meant Clark must have been driving very fast.

As I asked the question, their immediate reaction was what you see when people know something you don't know but don't want to be the one to tell you. There were those quick glances back and forth between them that seem to say, "You tell him! Why me? You should tell him!" Finally I broke the silence and asked that one of them please tell me the truth.

The answer that finally came was not one I wanted to hear. One of them had talked to some eyewitnesses, or should I say "participants" in the evening's events. The accident was caused by much more than driving carelessly or wet conditions on a country road. Clark was struggling for his life because he had been racing.

As painful as it was to hear what they knew about the accident, I didn't doubt it was true. It explained why so many classmates were there at the hospital that I had never met before. Drag racing had become part of the school culture – a social event – and word of the crash had spread quickly. No doubt some of them had been at the hospital simply out of curiosity while others were genuinely sorry that things had gone so wrong.

The report of the race also explained another thing which had been going on before Saturday night. Several weeks earlier, Clark told us he wanted to join a "car club" with a few of his buddies.

He was in the phase of having a car for the first time that many of us have gone through. You remember – that desire to shine it up and fix it up to the best of your ability. I can remember having a Volkswagen Beetle when I was sixteen that didn't have enough power to hardly make it out of the driveway but I was proud of it and changed out every part I could find. I put new tires on it, a new radio in it, new floor mats and even did some work on the engine even though I had no real clue what I was doing. I suppose it's just a guy thing.

This car club had gotten together several times at the local Taco Bell to pop the hoods, show off the shiny wax jobs and sit around and talk about who had ordered what part for their carburetor. They were even in the process of getting a decal made for their club that they each were going to proudly display on their rear windows – complete with a logo they had designed.

Two nights before the accident he had asked if it would be okay to go with the club to a church parking lot near one of the member's homes. I know that you're probably thinking "How clueless could you be?" Well, not totally. Even though Clark had asked permission, never been late for his curfew and never given me any real reason to not trust him, I was suspicious.

My concern was that talk would give way to some demonstrations or "joy rides" and those joy rides might lead to driving too fast. I remember sitting at a side road just a few blocks from the church one night for thirty minutes thinking, "If he drives by here going over the speed limit, then I'll make my point by taking his keys and parking his car for a while." But nobody drove by.

I spent the next two nights driving past where they said they would be for a couple of hours each night. Every time I was in sight of the church parking lot, they were doing exactly what they said they would be doing – popping their hoods, kicking their tires and talking about cars. Clark never knew I was there and he returned at 9:30 both nights, excited to tell us about what they had done.

Tonight I hadn't gone to check out the car club. Instead, I was at home when the phone rang. Tonight something had happened that had changed a social gathering into a deadly challenge. Some other students from Clark's high school had heard about the club getting together. It's still not clear to me if they were part of another rival club or were just there for the purpose of challenging someone to a race. Regardless of their motives, the outcome of their visit was a death defying drag race.

Most of the boys in Clark's club drove older model cars. They were renovation projects in the making. Clark's car might have been the only exception. Even though it was small and inexpensive, it was fairly new and needed no mechanical adjustments. The boys themselves were mostly from Clark's "gamer" crowd and pretty much kept to themselves at school, like all groups of teens tend to do. But on that Saturday night, someone had shown up driving a BMW and proudly parked it in the midst of the cars of the club. No work in progress there.

I can picture in my mind what happened next. What started out as a polite "nice car" turned into a "mine's better than yours" argument. Before anyone could cool down, the testosterone started to flow and a challenge to race was issued.

I mentioned earlier Clark has always been a bit timid and never liked adventure, so he would have been the last person I would have thought would get behind the wheel for a race. But one thing I failed to mention is that he is tremendously competitive. I believe his competitive spirit, along with the fact that his Lancer was newer than most of the cars in the car club, set in motion the events of that night.

Once the challenge to drag race had been accepted, a decision was made - either on the basis of fairness or, as bizarre as it may sound, for safety reasons - to balance the load in the two cars.

My heart suddenly began to feel the same sense of panic it had felt hours before. Because now I was sitting there in the emergency waiting room, hearing for the first time that Clark had not been alone in the car that night. Two other boys from his high school – neither of them close friends nor part of the car club – were in the car as it disintegrated around the utility pole.

On this dark, rainy night I hadn't witnessed a miracle of God. No, I was seeing the miracles of God. Perhaps none of them were more mighty, and in the end more for Clark's protection, than the miracle that those two boys lived. In fact, we learned the next day that the boys were treated at a local hospital and released the same night with injuries that were not life threatening. One of the boys had a facial fractures caused by colliding with Clark's head when the passenger seat bolts broke away from the frame due to the force of the impact. His seat actually became airborne.

The other young man fractured his thumb. His injury came from sitting in the back seat, gripping the headrest in front of him as the car "exploded" around him. He would tell me months later that in the seconds following the impact, he thought he had died.

Our story could have been one of so much more tragedy if it had not been for the Lord protecting those young men that night. Living with the consequences that Clark's decision had caused in his own life was hard enough. But to live with severely injuring or killing someone else by that decision would have been more than any of us could bear.

# Finding Grace

*"And God is able to make all grace abound toward you, that you, always having all sufficiency in all things, may have an abundance for every good work."*
*2 Corinthians 9:8 (NKJV)*

Telling Debbie and our family what I had just learned about the accident was so hard. How much more could we take in the middle of our unbelievable night? Not only was our son clinging to life on an hour by hour basis, but he brought this on himself with one terribly irresponsible decision. He had also risked the life of two other kids. Would they be alright? Was there a way we could have prevented this?

I remember looking at Clark's grandfather after I shared the cause of the accident. Delbert had worked hard for over forty years as a brick mason at the local steel mill. He never called in sick and was never late his entire career. He built his own home. He and Debbie's mother had raised four children on one salary. If you look up responsibility in the dictionary, my father-in-law's picture will probably be there.

When I glanced at his face, I expected to see a look of disappointment at best and disgust at worst. Clark had done all this to himself by being what his Pappaw had never been – irresponsible. Instead I saw a look I wasn't expecting. It was a look of grace. It was a look of love and forgiveness. I know that's what it was because I saw it over and over again in the months to come. No single person would be more responsible for us being able to bring Clark home than his grandfather.

I know it's hard to accept rejection and abandonment, but it's sometimes harder to accept grace. One of the simple definitions you always hear for the word grace is "receiving something you don't deserve". We received a lot of grace that night and in the months to come and it became very humbling. We received it from our family. We received it from our friends. We received it from our church. We received it from the families of the boys who were in the car that night. We received it from government officials. Over and over in our lives we received encouragement when we expected condemnation. And we needed every bit of it.

Our long night was really just beginning. Another knock at the waiting room door brought news Clark was on his way to the PICU. They told us it would be at least another hour before he was settled and we could see him. Since it was past 3 AM, we sent everyone home because there was nothing more they could do. Everybody finally left except for one of Debbie's best friends and co-workers, Jo Ann. She had met us at the hospital and been with us the entire time.

The three of us spent the next ninety minutes outside what would become our new home for the next three weeks – the Pediatric Intensive Care Unit. We were so anxious to be able to see Clark that it seemed as if time stood still. I would glance at the clock, thinking ten or fifteen minutes had gone only to see that five or six had ticked off. After the projected one hour had passed we couldn't help but worry even more. Was something wrong? Had something happened and they weren't telling us?

Somehow Jo Ann was able to calm Debbie down through the wait. She reminded her how long it took to do admission paperwork or get results back from the lab or get IVs started.

These were things that they did together every day and the reminders helped.

Around 5AM someone finally came out and told us that we could go back to see him. I quickly got up and started for the doorway when Debbie stopped me and turned to Jo Ann to ask another favor. "Would you please go in first and take a look at how they have things set up?" she asked. Jo Ann was more than willing to help and headed through the doors with the nurse. I was a bit stunned. We had been outside those doors for nearly two hours just waiting for that invitation to come. I thought I would have to run to keep up with my wife when the time came to see Clark. But deep inside her the battle was still raging between the nurse and Mom. She wisely sent another nurse in – one whose professional opinion she could trust completely – to do the kind of evaluation that a mother shouldn't have to do. She was looking for the calming reassurance that he was being treated with medical excellence. That would free her up to focus on being just a Mom and also prevent another clash like we had been through with the trauma surgeon just hours before.

In just a few short minutes, Jo Ann rejoined us and reported that Clark was receiving the best care possible. She started down the list of all the technical jargon with Debbie and I could see my wife was becoming calmer. They were going through the Debbie's mental checklist. When the report was finished, we told the nurse we were ready to see Clark. As the doors opened and we started to walk down the hallway, it seemed so strange to be passing rooms filled with baby beds and see toddlers asleep. We were on the way to see our 6'1", 215-pound son and he was right next to a small infant.

I firmly believe Clark's assignment to the PICU was a special part of God's plan for both Clark and us. The unit was staffed with a physician on the floor during the entire dayshift. This resulted in a level of care far better than the care he would have been given on any adult unit. We also were given better care too. The PICU allowed both parents to remain with their child as long as they wanted to each day. In an adult unit we would have been forced to observe strict visiting hours.

When we got near his room, I didn't have any fear about what I would see when I went through the door. After all, I had seen him in the ER just moments after he arrived and it couldn't be any worse. I was so wrong.

Maybe it was because we had been up now for nearly twenty-four hours or perhaps it was the dim lighting in the room and the darkness outside, but walking in the room seemed like walking into a morgue. As we looked at him lying there our hearts sank again. My wife buried her head into my chest and she began to sob uncontrollably. We stood there and held each other, wiping away the tears. We needed the Lord's strength now more than ever.

Clark looked pale and cold and so lifeless. Every breath filling his lungs with oxygen was being supplied by a machine. His arms laid motionless out to his sides with IVs in each one which were attached to multiple pumps – each one with its own sequence of beeps and clicks. Every heartbeat was recorded as a blip on a monitor above his bed. Coming out of both rib cages were tubes draining blood into bags clipped to the bedrails. His eyes were starting to show bruising and there was a cut above his left temple.

We just stood there dazed for a few minutes and then we leaned over and started talking to him - letting him know we were there with him and that most importantly God was with him. We would do that a lot over the next weeks. We both gently kissed his forehead.

The nurse who worked so hard to get him settled started to explain each device hooked up to him. She knew Debbie was a RN, so she communicated in their lingo and asked Debbie what questions she might have. We were so impressed by the care and compassion we were shown by the entire PICU staff at the Cabell-Huntington Hospital.

After the nurse left us alone with Clark, Debbie asked me to go to the waiting room and bring Jo Ann back to see him again. They spent some time looking at each IV pump, each wound, every bruise and sizing up the situation together. Having received this final gift from Jo Ann, we sent her home to get some rest and then prepared to follow up our long night with an even longer day.

We only had an hour before the nursing shift change during which time we were required to leave the unit. It was the only short period of time that parents were asked to leave. So for that first hour we just sat silently and watched. We watched every movement up and down of his chest. We watched every heartbeat on the monitor. We watched the readout of his body temperature. We watched every drip of fluid that transferred from a pump into his IV tubing.

The only thing that broke our vigil was when we felt the need to stand by the bed and check him again from head to toe. In that first hour we memorized every cut and bruise on his body. Debbie started picking yellow paint specks out of his hair and off his skin – a project that would take her days to complete.

Finally the shift change began and we went to the PICU waiting area. We were only able to sit there for a few minutes because it reminded us too much of the two hours of uncertainty we had experienced there earlier in the night. So we walked down the hallway and found some vending machines. Neither of us wanted anything to eat at the moment but we knew we at least had to drink something in order to keep going.

I think it's probably the same for anyone who goes through an emergency situation. In that first calm moment after the immediate crisis is past, it hits you. Your mind starts to buzz with all kinds of questions. How are we going to manage this? Who do we need to call? What about work? Who's going to feed the dog? Everything in your life is suddenly on hold but it's not. Life all around you keeps going while you're frozen in time. Of all the help that people offered, that immediate "I'll take care of it for you" was the most important.

We had one area of concern that outweighed all the rest. Since the beginning of the school year, we had been hosting a foreign exchange student named Andrey. He was from the country of Kyrgyzstan near Russia and was scheduled to leave for home in a week. He and Clark had become very close throughout the year. Since Clark's an only child it was his first time to have somebody around all the time and he loved it. All the other concerns could probably be handled with a phone call or an adjustment to somebody's schedule but the thought of moving Andrey to another home that was unfamiliar to him was weighing heavily upon us.

That weight was soon lifted by two of Clark's best friends from our church. Paul and Brandon were more than just friends. They were a part of our family. They were both at our house multiple times a week – for sure every Sunday and Wednesday night. I had even given them a number in our family. Rather than call one Son #2 and the other Son #3, I just averaged it together and called them both Son #2.5.

They had both been at the hospital until 2AM and then had gone back to our house to spend the night with Andrey. Without us even having to ask, they sent word the next day that they would move into our house for the next week and take care of Andrey. They would get him to school, to the store, to track practice – they would be his brothers. And as an added bonus they would feed the dog too! Now that's being true friends.

Most importantly they said they would bring Andrey to see Clark when the time was right. We just prayed that would be possible before he had to return home. God answered that prayer in just a few short days as Paul, Brandon and Andrey came to the hospital together. We were worried it would be hard on Andrey emotionally to never see Clark again but walking into Clark's room was more disturbing than we expected. Andrey had never been in a hospital before in his native country of Kyrgyzstan, let alone an intensive care unit.

As the boys arrived with him, he timidly stood in the hallway behind them until we reassured him that it was alright to enter the room. He stood at the end of the bed silently for a few minutes and then began to ask questions about the equipment that was delivering life support to Clark's body. Andrey was extremely intelligent and needed a frame of reference to understand what was happening. Finally he asked how badly Clark was injured. We explained what we knew and told him that it would take a miracle from the Lord for Clark to live. Andrey stood there silently looking at Clark for a few more minutes and then tears began to run down his cheeks. He hugged us both and quietly walked out of the room. It was the last time Debbie would see him.

As Debbie and I returned from the vending machines we had no idea what the day would bring. We called the PICU desk and were told that we were welcome to return back to Clark's room. As we came through the door we met his day shift nurse, Lenda. She would be his nurse for those first three days and we immediately formed a bond with her. Lenda was an experienced nurse who was filled with optimism and energy. She always seemed happy and committed to do whatever it took to make Clark - or us - more comfortable and cared for.

Never was that commitment more tested than about an hour into the first day. She received orders that Clark was to be transported back down to the CT lab for another scan to check the bleeding on his brain. She worked so hard to get Clark ready to go. There were critical IV lines to readjust. He had to be transported with the respirator and monitors. His neck was still in a brace because the x-rays taken the night before had not been able to determine if he had fractured any of his vertebrae.

It took five nurses, Debbie and I over an hour just to get him down a fifty foot hallway and onto an elevator. At one point I looked over at Lenda as she was holding his neck still while the bed was being moved out the door. Sweat was pouring off her forehead. But she never uttered one word of complaint. None of the staff did. They just pitched in and took care of him.

It took only a few minutes to do the second CT scan and then we turned to make the return trip. Once we got Clark settled back in his room, we could all breathe a sigh of relief. The staff got a few minutes of a much needed break and Debbie went back to removing yellow specs of paint. The results would take several hours to get back. So we did what we learned to do very well - wait.

# Mother's Day

As we settled down for our first day in the PICU, Lenda was taking care of us too. She brought us an extra reclining chair and made sure we had pillows and blankets. She even ordered a couple of lunch trays that were a welcome surprise.

In spite of her continuous work in our room, we soon noticed a quietness to the unit. There weren't very many people walking the hallways. There were only a couple of people at the nursing station and only one doctor, also a trauma surgeon from the ER, had been in to check on Clark that morning. Then it dawned on us – it's Sunday morning. And it wasn't just any Sunday, it was Mother's Day.

I didn't mention it to Debbie all day long but I knew she was thinking about it. She had lost her Mother two years earlier and mine had passed away six years before. At least we didn't have to bring up the subject of cancelling plans with family.

Clark had purchased some gifts for her and had been hiding them until the "big day". When we finally got to go home, I found them wrapped in his closet. They stayed there for the next year. When I told Debbie they were there, she refused to open them until Clark could give them to her himself.

Since that day, we've been a family that always gets presents early. We've instituted what we call a "no waiting policy". It doesn't matter if it's Christmas or your birthday. When somebody in our family makes their gift selection you receive it the same day. We don't want any more wrapped presents in the closet in case tomorrow never comes. We don't use it as an excuse to throw all caution to the wind or become impulsive. We just cherish every day that we have together and celebrate early!

Even though it was Mother's Day Sunday, Clark's condition was critical and everyone was focused on improving it. By mid-morning we got a visit from the neurosurgeon on call for the weekend, Dr. Weinzweig. He was a very quiet, gentle guy and, as you might imagine, very intelligent. He had come from seeing Clark's CT scans and wanted us to know what Clark was facing. The second scan had shown that there was still active bleeding going on in the brain.

The ventricles, or open spaces, in his brain were filled with blood. Since these areas normally contain spinal fluid, the addition of the blood was creating pressure on the inside of his skull. As the pressure builds, it cannot move the bone of the skull, so it starts to push on the brain tissue itself. The result would be the loss of that brain tissue – forever. Once it was lost, it could not be regenerated. The best scenario would be loss of certain cognitive or physical functions. The worst would be death.

With the cranial pressure continuously increasing, he recommended the insertion of a "bolt" into Clark's skull. It would involve drilling a small hole in the skull and inserting a catheter that would allow blood and spinal fluid to drain and hopefully relieve the pressure. I'm sure we must have looked very hopeful because Dr. Weinzwieg quickly brought us back down to earth. He warned us the bolt would typically work for twenty-four to forty-eight hours before becoming clotted with blood. It was only a short-term solution. But short-term or not, we understood the need for the relief and gave our consent on the spot. They asked us to step out for a few minutes and performed the procedure at the bedside.

We had been on such a rollercoaster ride emotionally. He's alive when we get to the car – they can't get him out soon enough

— he makes it to the ER and needs no surgery for internal organ damage — he has a massive head injury — he's made it to the morning — he may die from the pressure on his brain. We felt more and more like emotional yoyos, so all we knew to do with each swing of emotion was pray. We prayed for Clark and Dr. Weinzweig as he inserted the bolt. We prayed that God would help us to trust Him with it all.

We decided at that point that we would use a reminder about faith that Debbie taught me several weeks before. She was participating in a Bible study with some of the ladies at our church. It was Beth Moore's *Believing God* study. She loved it and learned a great deal, but they were only three weeks into it when the accident happened. One of the things Beth Moore chose to do in the study was to develop a teaching tool to help the participants memorize five principles. Each time they said a principle, they were to hold out their hand and raise up one of their fingers. It was more than simply counting to five. It was done in a very firm way almost letting your fingers "declare" the principle.

As I mentioned, Debbie had only been through the first three weeks but they were the three weeks that we needed the most. With the thumb held up she would repeat the first principle of "God is who He says He is." The index finger would declare that, "God can do what He says He can do." The third finger represented "I am who God says I am."

I suppose I should offer a little bit of explanation at this point about my spiritual and vocational backgrounds. I had been pastoring for twenty-three years in Southern Baptist churches ranging from church plants in northern Ohio to traditional, established churches in the South.

I am very conservative theologically. I am a biblical inerrantist. I received my Master of Divinity and Doctor of Ministry degrees at Southeastern Baptist Theological Seminary in Wake Forest, NC. I am doctrinally, emotionally and psychologically about as far away from being classified a "charismatic" as one could be.

But above all the labels someone might put on me, I think they would put "He believes God" pretty high on the list. Now it was time to put up or shut up.

Did I really believe God is who the Bible reveals him to be? The God who created everything that is? The God who brought about miracle after miracle in peoples' lives? I had heard and read about those miracles but I had never experienced one personally.

Did I really believe God would do something in our situation? Of course I believed that he "could" do what he promised, but did he promise us Clark would live? I wanted to hear from God.

Did I really believe I am who God says I am? That was maybe the toughest. I was brought up with the "I'm just a sinner saved by grace" concept crammed down my throat almost exclusively. So I had a general feeling I shouldn't expect good things from God because I was being blessed far more than I deserved just by waking up today. But I was slowly learning that God loves me because I am his child – warts and all. I was finally believing God loved me in spite of my wrong decisions and sinful choices. In fact, he loves me more than I love my son who's dying in the other room because of his decisions. I was not going to give up on Clark or love him any less, so why did I think I was a better Father than my Heavenly Father?

So as we waited for the procedure in Clark's room to finish, we flashed those signs to each other. God is who he says he is… God can do what he says he can do…I am who God says I am. We were starting to believe God in a whole new way.

The procedure went well but the insertion of the "bolt" added a whole new level anxiety for me. We were glad it could help relieve some of the pressure on Clark's brain but it came with a downside. It was designed to relieve the pressure but it would monitor the pressure as well. That monitor was displayed right above the head of Clark's bed alongside all the other vital signs they were tracking.

The doctor told us the normal range is zero to ten. Clark's pressure needed to be maintained under a reading of twenty to insure more brain damage was not caused by the swelling. As we walked back into the room after talking with the doctor, my eyes immediately found the monitor. It read fourteen.

I suppose there's a psychological reason why you tend to fixate on something when you're under the kind of stress we were experiencing. For me, the focus of my attention and prayer became that monitor. I couldn't take my eyes off of it for hours at a time. It was constantly changing – fourteen – thirteen – twelve – fourteen - fifteen. With every change in that number I could feel my whole body either relax or tense up and that went on hour after hour after hour.

Tied directly to my tension, however, was my prayer. We read in 1 Thessalonians 5:17 that we are to "Pray without ceasing." I had no idea what that really meant until that day. Now with every change of that number I found myself either thanking God it went down or asking God to intervene so it wouldn't go any higher.

For the rest of Sunday, we only saw one other specialist and that was an orthopedic surgeon named Dr. Giangarra, or "Dr. G" as we came to call him. I'm not sure why, but he became the most personally attached to Clark of all the doctors and specialists we would see over the next few months. He stopped in almost daily to check on Clark's progress.

At this early stage he was monitoring the broken left femur but told us he was limited on what he could do. Eventually it would require surgery to heal properly, but as Dr. G put it, "That's way down on the list of things to worry about right now." So early that evening, two nurses came by the room and started to add the additional equipment to Clark's hospital bed that was necessary to put Clark's leg in traction.

As the sun went down on that first day in the PICU, we were exhausted. We had been awake for nearly forty hours with very little to eat. But we just couldn't bear to leave his side – and I couldn't stop watching that monitor. So the nursing staff got us some fresh blankets and pillows and we settled into the chairs as best we could. . I remember fighting going to sleep because I needed to keep praying for that number to stay under twenty.

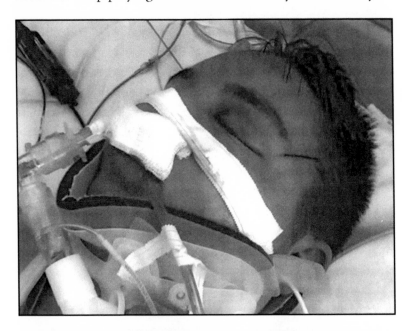

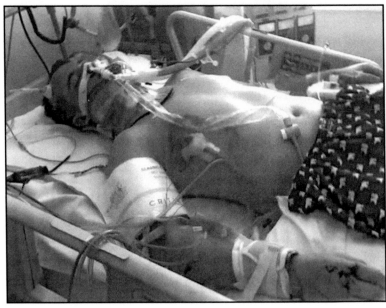

# Now We Wait...

*"But those who wait on the Lord shall renew their strength; They shall mount up with wings like eagles, They shall run and not be weary, They shall walk and not faint."*
*Isaiah 40:31 (NKJV)*

At 7AM the next morning it became obvious the weekend was over. Traffic in the hallways of the PICU had definitely increased as people from many different departments in the hospital began to see the patients. Various technicians passed by our room pushing equipment to take x-rays, give breathing treatments and do physical therapy. Lenda came through our door for day two just a few minutes after the start of the shift. As she looked over Clark's chart, she seemed pleased with the things that had happened on Sunday evening, which gave us both some reassurance.

As Lenda started to make adjustments on Clark's IV pumps, a new face walked through the door. It was a slender, middle-aged male face with wire rimmed glasses and pepper colored hair parted in the middle. It was a face that beamed confidence and decisiveness. As I stood up to greet this new face, Lenda introduced us to Dr. Eduardo Pino, one of two Pediatric Intensivists who oversaw the patients in the PICU. He was beginning his two week rotation to the unit where he would be present each day during the entire day shift to care for the needs of the children.

We would come to lean upon Dr. Pino for strength, encouragement and honesty over and over again. He was kind, compassionate, straight to the point and never seemed in a hurry. There were days he would be in Clark's room four or five times to examine him or make adjustments to his care.

As he came in and said hello to us, it was clear he was already up to speed on Clark's progress since Saturday night. He first sat down and began to review the results of the tests Clark had been through. One bit of good news that morning was that the radiologists had ruled out any fractures of the neck or spine. What a miracle in and of itself! They would remove the neck brace later that morning.

After he examined Clark that first day, he sat back down and talked to us about the reality of traumatic brain injuries. I had never experienced someone with this type of injury before and didn't know what to expect. Debbie, of course, had cared for and transported patients with head injuries but had never cared for them long-term.

In his honest way, Dr. Pino told us several things we needed to hear. The first was Clark's life was still very much in danger. While he was stabilizing with the treatment, things could change suddenly. The second was there were no "textbook" outcomes for brain injury patients. He talked with us about what Clark might be like "if" he regained consciousness. He could wake up and be violent and belligerent. He might not know who we were. He might have severe mental and physical disabilities.

But the most important thing he told us that day was that nobody could know what would happen for sure. As long as Clark was alive and progressing there was hope. Each brain injury patient responded differently and all we could do was to wait and see. It's the only time in my life I have ever been excited about what a doctor didn't know.

We grew to look forward to Dr. Pino's daily visits. They would usually include some news about improvements in Clark's vital signs or a blood work report he could say was a positive sign. They usually ended with the reminder of "now we wait and see" that somehow he always seemed to make believable.

But the middle of his visit each day was not something we looked forward to in the least. During his physical exam of Clark he would test for what he called a "response to pain stimulus". It's one of the body's reflex actions and it gives some indication the brain is still functioning.

So each day he would take a non-sharp object and rub it up the soles of Clark's feet or pinch some skin on his arm or chest. But there was no response. No flinching. No subconscious reaction to defend against the pain. Nothing. Day after day there was no response – except Dr.Pino's "We'll just wait and see tomorrow."

The message of waiting was starting to get our attention. I suppose I had seen far too many episodes of *Little House on the Prairie* or *Lassie* where someone was in a coma. According to those shows you're supposed to sit by their bedside and hold their hand until they suddenly wake up and announce they are hungry! Isn't that the way it happens? Well, our miracle didn't happen quite that way.

God was trying to tell us through the people around us we needed to wait on him to work in his own time. Looking back I can see God's reasoning for not delivering that instant miracle. Clark's body was bruised and broken and thankfully unresponsive to pain. I can't imagine the type of excruciating pain he would have felt if he had been conscious.

But waiting is so hard to do, especially if you have no idea about how long you have to wait or what you're waiting for. We were at a point now where we needed a word from God about the future. So the Lord began to send people into our lives to remind us about the promises in His Word and about his love for us.

The first vivid reminder came from Jo Ann, the friend and nurse who had been with us through the whole first night ordeal. She came to visit Clark and just sit and talk to us for a while. Before she left, she said she had been praying for us and a particular Bible verse came to mind she was supposed to share. It was Jeremiah 29:11 and she quoted it to us from the New International Version – "For I know the plans I have for you," declares the Lord, "plans to prosper you and not to harm you, plans to give you hope and a future."

The second one came through a card we received from another of Debbie's friends who had been praying for us. She hadn't seen this friend in awhile but word had spread quickly in the first few days. The card also said that she felt strongly impressed by God to share a Bible verse as God's promise to us. It was from Psalm 118:17 where it says, "I shall not die, but live, and declare the works of the LORD."

For the next week we watched Dr. Pino come and go with no response from Clark. But now we were waiting in a different way – with a promise.

Those verses of Scripture had given us the only sense of hope we had experienced since it all began. I wish I could say it only took those two reminders from God that he loved us and was in control but I'd be lying if I did. We struggled every single day between worrying and believing. So to help us even more, God would send someone else to say or do something to meet our needs.

One of those people was Clark's night shift nurse for days three and four. Her name was Kristin. She was in her early twenties and was full of compassion for the kids she took care of. She was one of those people who you feel comfortable around from the first moment you meet them.

Debbie has a keen sense of discernment about people and she trusted Kristin almost immediately. Kristin would come in regularly to check on Clark and as time allowed, she and Debbie would talk about nursing and about Clark's accident.

For the first two days, neither of us had left Clark's room. But on the third day we realized we couldn't take care of him if we didn't take care of ourselves. Our niece had made a run to our house for clothes and supplies, so we decided to get a room at a nearby hotel and split the days. One of us would sleep while the other stayed at the hospital around the clock.

The only exceptions to that arrangement were the nights Kristin was Clark's nurse. I remember that on Kristin's second shift I started to leave for the motel. Debbie looked at me and said, "I'm going with you. Clark will be fine with Kristin." I was shocked. We both left that night to get some much needed rest and a break from it all. God had again provided someone just at the right time to help meet our needs.

The first night away from Clark was extremely difficult. We were exhausted in every imaginable way. Our bodies needed sleep and our hearts and minds needed rest. But how do you turn your mind off in a time of crisis? We prayed for him before going to bed and then tried to get some sleep. The key word here is "tried". All we seemed to accomplish was to dwell on thoughts of how he was doing and what the future would hold. I think we called Kristin three times that night and each time she assured us her "little buddy" was still stable and well taken care of. So we slept for an hour here and there and finally decide to shower and return to the hospital a little after six the next morning.

As we were getting ready, I walked over to the desk in the hotel room and picked up the cards we had received. I started reading again the scripture promises people had been sharing. At that point Debbie finally broke down and began to sob. I walked over to her and wrapped my arms around as she let go of the emotions she had been holding back. After a few minutes, she walked over to the desk and picked up one of the cards I had been reading to her just a few minutes before. She startled me as she threw the card on the table. Then she made a desperate statement that really was a prayer. She yelled, "I want my own verse! I don't want to hear what God is saying to everybody else. I need to hear it from him myself!"

With that declaration, she reached over and picked up the Gideon Bible which had been placed in the room and desperately flung it on the table. She grabbed at a page, peeled it open and began to read. She read silently for less than a minute and then she began to sob again. But with the tears there was a smile this time. She wildly motioned me over to her and pointed down at the page she had been reading. Choking back the tears, she managed to cry out, "Look!", as she pointed down. Debbie had randomly opened the Bible to the seventh chapter of Luke, or perhaps I should more accurately say the Bible had opened itself to the following verses:

*11 Now it happened, the day after, that He went into a city called Nain; and many of His disciples went with Him, and a large crowd. 12 And when He came near the gate of the city, behold, a dead man was being carried out, the only son of his mother; and she was a widow. And a large crowd from the city was with her. 13 When the Lord saw her, He had compassion on her and said to her, "Do not weep." 14 Then He came and touched the open coffin, and those who carried him stood still. And He said, "Young man, I say to you, arise." 15 So he who was dead sat up and began to speak. And He presented him to his mother. (NKJV)*

God had answered another mother's prayer. He had spoken to Debbie from His Word! It's hard to be able to describe it but we both felt from that moment on Clark was not going to die. We were now able to raise the thumb and the index finger as reminders to each other – God is who he says he is AND God can do what he says he will do. We still didn't know how long we would have to wait but now we had a sense of what we were waiting for. Somewhere there would be a light at the end of our tunnel and we would see what only God could do.

We were becoming more and more aware we were waiting on God but we were not waiting alone. He already knew what we needed before we were aware of it and he was working his plan for a hope and a future.

# The 4th Man In The Car

As we waited, the days turned into nearly a week. God had used a doctor, a nurse, a friend and a card to encourage us each step of the way. Now it was time for him to use a voice. That voice would be the final turning point for our believing God.

Before that voice was heard, God had already begun to prepare us for the message. Two major milestones had been reached in Clark's recovery on the previous day. The first came during Dr. Pino's daily visit. He had given us the progress report, ordered some changes of Clark's treatment and began Clark's physical exam.

Finally after days of waiting and watching, Dr. Pino reached down and rubbed Clark's sternum with his knuckles. Clark's left hand slowly moved towards his chest! It was the first movement since the accident. With a wide smile on his face, he said, "That's great" and he strolled out of the room.

The second came later in the day. We were scheduled for a new CT scan. This would be Clark's third and the first one since Sunday when it was discovered he was still actively bleeding. It was still quite the ordeal to transport him but they were able to obtain a portable ventilator, which made it much easier.

Dr. Weinzweig had ordered the test to see if the bolt might be removed, so his associate, Dr. Ignatiadus was actually in the technician's room to read the scan immediately. After they removed Clark from the scanner, they held us up at the doorway to give the doctor a moment to evaluate things.

He stepped out from the darkened room just a few steps and in his Mediterranean accent said, "It looks good. Ninety percent of the blood has been reabsorbed by the body. I think we can remove the bolt today." Before he could finish his sentence, Debbie rushed up to him and gave him this huge hug that practically scared him to death! She said, "Thank you, thank you" over and over. He just smiled and nodded.

God is who he says he is! The bolt which was expected to function for two days drained for over a week. Clark's cranial pressure never exceeded his age of sixteen.

God had even prepared Clark for this moment months before. In the summer before the accident our church had sponsored a visit from a Christian weightlifting ministry called the Power Team. Clark got to spend some time around them and their influence inspired him to begin lifting weights and working out.

By the time May rolled around he had really "buffed up". At times I heard him kidding around with the high school football players that he was lifting more than they could with his massive legs (definitely not from my side of the family!). Now on this critical day, the explanation they were giving us for the change in the CT scan was Clark's muscle mass had provided the circulation needed to reabsorb such quantities of blood.

As all of us returned him to his room, the nurses kept saying, "That's so great!" But it was more than great to us. God was doing what he said he would do. He did have plans for Clark.

We truly believed it but we soon would find ourselves in the same mindset as a parent mentioned in the Bible. In Mark chapter nine, a man brought his very sick son to Jesus. The Dad said to Jesus, "If You can do anything, have compassion on us and help us." Jesus said to him, "If you can believe, all things *are* possible to him who believes." Immediately the father of the child cried out and said with tears, "Lord, I believe; help my unbelief!" That's exactly where we were.

In spite of the two very positive changes in Clark's condition, we were still overwhelmed by the negatives. He had flinched once to the pain but hadn't moved an inch at any other time. He was not responsive to commands or any other stimulus. We were so thankful to see the bolt and the monitor go but now he had developed an unexplained daily fever. The theory was the fever was neurologically induced but there was also the chance of some infection somewhere. So multiple times a day they drew blood cultures. And as long as Clark ran a fever, they could not do surgery on his leg. So back and forth we went. The rollercoaster continued to run.

Then one week to the day of the accident, God spoke through the voice I mentioned earlier. It was Saturday morning about 10:30 and a very dear friend from out of town came to see Clark. Since the PICU only allowed one visitor and one parent back in the room, I decided I would take a break and walk out of the unit and down the hallway to the vending machines.

As I went through the ICU waiting area, I heard the pay phone ringing. It seems there's always one in any waiting room and it's always ringing. Usually I ignored it because I didn't want to waste the time I could be spending with Clark. But this morning I decided I would be a little more Christian about it and answer the phone. I figured I would say hello, yell for some family who probably wasn't there and then politely hang it back up.

So I picked up the receiver and said my "Hello". To my amazement a woman's voice on the other end said, "I'm trying to reach the Menshouse family". I told her who I was and then she reluctantly began to share with me why she had called.

Her husband operated the towing service which was called to remove the car from the crash site (what was left of it). She told me she was a Christian and she had been praying for Clark since the time the towing call came in, which by that time had been seven days.

I thanked her and expected to update her on his condition and hang up. But then she told me she had a message for us – from God. I know. I thought the same thing. Here's some nutcase who calls people and supposedly then gives them some mystical message that's supposed to make everything all better.

But as I heard her speak, I knew she wasn't making it up. Her voice had a nervousness, or maybe I would say a reverence, to it. I could tell she didn't do this type of thing on a regular basis so I listened intently.

She said "I'm to tell you that just as there was a fourth man in the fiery furnace with Shadrach, Meshach and Abednigo, so there was a fourth man in the car with the boys that night. He was protecting the other two boys and your son. He's been with your son since the moment of the accident and your son is going to be alright".

Then she added, "And I also have a message for your wife. Tell her God says this will not be the worst Mother's Day in her life but it will be the best. That just as God gave Abraham his son back, God gave her son back to her that day."

I thanked her for her kind words of encouragement and she interrupted me and said, "You don't understand. This isn't from me. God spoke to me and told me to call you and tell you this!" In that moment I felt God's spirit letting me know this wasn't some random call. I told her I would look forward to bringing Clark to meet her someday.

When I did finally meet her, nearly a year later, I was even more in awe of what God had done. She related to me the rest of the story. She said she had felt led by God to make the call days earlier but she struggled with what I would think and if I would believe her. She questioned herself about was it really God telling her to do this or just an idea of her own.

Finally she laid out a challenge to the Lord. She told God she would call the waiting room only once. If I answered the phone then she would know that the message really was from God and she would deliver the message. Every time I think about that moment I am in awe of the love and power of God.

I could never express in words how much strength this moment gave us. God had moved the heart of someone we had never met to give us a message about our crisis. It confirmed He loved us and He was in control. Even more it reminded us He loved Clark and was there with him from the very first moment. It was going to be alright. God had said so.

# When It Rains...

*All you need to remember is that God will never let you down;*
*he'll never let you be pushed past your limit; he'll always be there*
*to help you come through it.*
*1 Corinthians 10:13 (MSG)*

When it rains it pours? Right? Well, we certainly had experienced our share of rain – buckets full. But that's not the only way to finish that sentence, is it? Sometimes when it rains there are rainbows.

We had come so far in a week's time and yet we knew we had so far to go. God had given us a promise Clark was going to make it through. He had given it to us in such a way that we couldn't miss it or misunderstand it. But as I said earlier, our story wasn't going to be running on a thirty minute episode of a TV drama. We were more the feature film length! There was not going to be an event where Clark would open his eyes and declare everything was suddenly "OK". Our journey was a long one and far from over.

We spent week two in a new room in the unit. Following the third CT scan the staff decided to move us to a room that had a little more space. Most of the other PICU patients had come and gone in the first week. Some of them were transferred to the pediatric floor and others were taken back to hospitals closer to their homes. We, on the other hand, were going to be staying a bit longer and they wanted us to be as comfortable as possible.

Clark was still unconscious and unresponsive and he continued to have a fever each day. They had done numerous blood cultures showed no infection. As Dr. Pino continued to look for an explanation, he became more concerned that Clark's ventilator could be a cause. One risk of a ventilator is the development of pneumonia, so he ordered x-rays and more breathing treatments and told us he hoped to be able to get him off the machine in a few short days. Each day that the fever continued was another day Dr. G couldn't do surgery on the broken femur. It just seemed like it would never end.

One evening at the beginning of the second week, God spoke to the heart of still another stranger. I had gone out to the lobby to change places with a friend who had come to see Clark. When I got there I noticed a young lady, with red-hair and in her early twenties, sitting with her head down and a couple of notebooks on her lap. Our friend was sitting beside her and when I approached them she said, "I think this girl is here to see you guys." I introduced myself and asked her if that were so.

She very hesitantly said she had felt impressed three separate times by God to come meet us and share her own story with us. Her brother knew Clark from school and she had been following the reports. I invited her and our friend back to another waiting room which was available to PICU families and went to Clark's room to get Debbie. I noticed, as we walked to the room, that our visitor had a slight limp.

Over the next hour we listened to her own account of battling through and recovering from a brain injury. Her name was Misty and she had been in an automobile accident in her senior year of high school. Misty's car had gone off the road and collided head on with a tree. She was also flown to Cabell and was in a coma for seventeen days. She gave me a newspaper article that talked about her accident and then her subsequent recovery.

She guided us through two picture albums which contained photos of her in the PICU as well as time she spent at a rehabilitation center for brain injury patients. After she showed us the albums she asked if it would be OK to pray with Clark. It was a special moment to listen in on that prayer. Who better to prayer for what you're going through than someone who has been through it themselves?

After Misty left that night, I noticed Debbie was more quiet than usual. As we talked about what was bothering her she broke down and began to cry. Misty's visit had encouraged her by allowing us to see someone who had gone through such similar circumstances and was now married and leading a normal life. But it had also discouraged her and made her afraid about the future. Neither of us had given any thought to whether Clark would need rehabilitation at a specialized hospital or institution. We were so focused on the day to day that we hadn't thought about the next month or the next year.

She was also beginning to worry about when she would have to return to work. I had been given the freedom to take whatever time I needed away from the church in order to take care of Clark. But Debbie was quickly using up her vacation days and only had a few left. And as if she needed more pressure on her, we carried our medical insurance through her employer. If she lost her job there would be no way we could continue the coverage.

It was a heavy, heavy burden. Even though God was continuing to send us reminders of his ability to take care of us, all we could see were the threats and discouragements of the enemy. So all we knew to do was cry awhile and pray awhile. We would take one day at a time and ask God to give us wisdom to make each decision along the way.

In fact, the very next day would be a day of both highs and lows. Clark had been on the ventilator for a week and a half and was still spiking fevers. So the decision was made that morning to take him off and see how he did breathing on his own. It was a scary time for us but we agreed it was an important step. They asked us to leave the unit and walk down the hallway for a few minutes. I needed a break and the room was very crowded with staff, so I walked out into the hallway. Debbie chose to stay and "oversee" this huge step in Clark's recovery.

Those "give us a few minutes" trips always seemed more like hours than minutes. I would pace for a while and then lean on something for a while - until the urge to pace again returned. When you're taking one of those pacing trips, every second brings another worried thought into your mind about "What's taking them so long". Finally word came that I could return to his room. He was fine and breathing on his own!

When I stepped back into his room it was awesome to see the large blue hose that had been in his mouth replaced by the thin tubing of oxygen under his nose. Momma was wiping his face with a washcloth. He looked so much more comfortable and we were thankful to not have to hear the sound of the machine anymore. The silence truly was golden.

Someone once said God's timing is never early or never late. He is always on time. While I know that's true, we might also add the devil's timing isn't bad either. Just as we had finally experienced a major move forward in Clark's recovery, a social worker walked in and asked to speak to us.

We chitchatted for a few minutes as she asked how we felt about the care we were receiving. She was genuinely very nice and seemed concerned about what we as parents needed too. But then she dropped the bombshell. She asked the very question we had been crying over the night before - "Have you considered what facility you will want Clark placed in when he is well enough to transport?" Debbie couldn't even look at her as she ran over a list of possible places ranging from near the hospital to several states away. I politely told her we would think about it and she left the room. All we could do was sit in silence. Was that what God had in store for Clark? How could we leave him somewhere we were not? How often could we see him? How long would he be there? All the fear and worry just came flooding back into our hearts.

As it got closer to evening time, I thought we had about had enough for the moment. There weren't very many times we both left the hospital at the same time, but I felt this was one of those times that we needed to get out. Some different surroundings and a chance to take our mind off of the things were in order.

So after begging for a while and doing some mild threatening, Debbie agreed to go with me to dinner. We gathered up some of our things and started the long walk to the parking lot. We were on the fifth floor of the hospital, so we had to take an elevator ride and walk through a couple of buildings.

As we got within a sight of the entrance we heard thunder and saw people scurrying to get inside as a downpour took place. It was a typical early summer storm which only lasted about 10 minutes, so we decided to wait it out. As we finally stepped out into the parking lot, the sun came out. Debbie punched me and pointed up to the sky.

I saw something I had never seen before and have never seen since. Not one rainbow but two bright, vivid rainbows stretched from one side of the horizon to the other. I immediately thought about how God gave Noah a rainbow in the Bible to remind him of a promise – and now we had two. Debbie hugged me, held up her thumb and said, "God is who he said he is…"

# "X" Marks The Spot

*"A friend loves you all the time,*
*and a brother helps in time of trouble."*
*Proverbs 17:17 (NCV)*

It was wonderful to be able to walk back into Clark's room after dinner and watch him breathe on his own. The medical staff was working very hard to move him along the path to physically recovering. With the ventilator gone there remained two major hurdles – the fever and the broken femur. It was still possible the condition of the leg was causing the fever, so a consult was set up the next morning with Dr. Giangarra.

It was decided we couldn't wait any longer to address the break. Clark's heart rate had been racing during the night and the doctors feared he was experiencing severe pain, even though he still had not regained consciousness. The surgery was scheduled for later in the day and x-rays were ordered to check the condition of the leg.

Having x-rays taken was nothing new for us. The radiology department would send up a mobile unit and the pictures were taken in Clark's room. We were practically on a first name basis with the techs. When they arrived they usually asked us to step out of the room to provide us some protection from exposure. So as they arrived that day, they pulled the curtain across the glass wall of his room and I stepped out into the hallway and leaned up against the wall by the nurse's station.

It only took a few minutes to get the pictures they wanted. When they were finished they pulled the curtains open. I was still walking in the hallway and glanced back over my shoulder into Clark's room. I immediately knew something was different but it took a second to realize what it was. When it hit me, I wanted to jump up and down in the hallway. For the first time since the accident, Clark had opened his eyes! The only time we had seen those wonderful, awesome hazel eyes in the last two weeks was when someone would pull back his eyelids and shine a light into them to check the dilation of his pupils.

As I rushed back into the room, I started talking to him somehow expecting he would answer back or at least nod in agreement when I told him we were there and we loved him. But there was nothing. I was somehow still expecting an instant miracle but it still wasn't happening the way I pictured it.

I'm often asked how long Clark was in a "coma" after the accident and I always hesitate to answer. Most of us think of a coma as total unconsciousness - almost like a sleep state. But that's not completely true. The real question is not if someone's eyes are open but if they are responsive? Can they respond to pain stimulus? Can they respond to your voice? Can they move on their own? The answer for Clark to all of those questions was still "no" and it would be that way for months to come.

I've described his condition this way: "The lights were on but nobody was home". Now don't get me wrong, it was progress for which we were so thankful. But it was also very, very strange and sad. Clark would stare blankly off into the distance but was in no way in contact with this world.

We didn't get to see his eyes open for very long because it was soon time to take him to surgery. Dr. G's original plan had been to insert a rod into the femur and join the two broken bones together. Such a surgery would provide the best opportunity for a full rehab of the leg. But with the fever still present, he felt it was too risky to introduce the rod into the bone. He feared we would be inviting infection to set in.

Instead, he devised a plan to insert a series of smaller rods perpendicular to the bone and then join them together on the outside of Clark's leg to align the femur. It's a device called an external fixator and it basically looks like a TV antenna! The mechanism became one of the most difficult things to manage during his rehabilitation but allowed the bone to heal perfectly aligned.

When Clark returned from surgery, he returned to his third room in the PICU. He was progressing in his recovery and did not require as much space so the room was made available to someone who needed it more. We had shed the ventilator and several IV pumps over the last few days. The only new piece of equipment which had been added was a feeding tube pump.

Now that the leg was stabilized, Dr. G ordered physical therapy to begin a more aggressive treatment plan. Clark still couldn't move on his own so the therapists worked on flexing his arms, legs and ankles. They hoped to keep the muscles, joints and tendons flexible and stop any deterioration due to lack of movement.

Dr. Giangarra's involvement with our family was nothing but positive. He always stopped by to visit Clark and encourage us, even when he knew it would be days before he could be more involved in Clark's treatment. Now that Clark had begun to open his eyes, Dr. G would always try and get some response before he left the room. He never left without saying, "Hey Clark! Give me a 'thumbs up'" and he would show the sign to Clark. When no response came back, he would just pat a foot and tell him he would see him again soon. It became sort of a daily routine for them.

As the third week in the PICU began, Clark's daily schedule was becoming more routine. The nursing staff had a little less to do and the therapists had a little more. Every morning we usually were paid a visit from Physical Therapy. One young lady had been to the room several times to work with Clark and had just finished the morning's stretching exercises.

As she started to leave, she also asked Clark for the "thumbs up" sign. Slowly his left hand began to move. We both watched him tuck his fingers under his palm to form a fist and then he moved his thumb away from his hand. It was the first sign of response to the outside world we had seen! It took days to see it repeated but I knew Clark was "in there" somewhere. There was somebody at home after all. Now the question was how to help him get out.

The news spread pretty fast through our new family of PICU staff. Dr. Pino, the nursing staff and many of the therapists tried to get him to repeat the event that day but with no success. Nevertheless everybody was happy with the news, especially Momma who had been at the motel asleep getting prepared for her stay during the night.

The only person who seemed disappointed was Dr. G! With a grin on his face he lectured Clark about showing favoritism to a pretty young therapist over him. Eventually, though, Dr. G would get his "thumbs up" and more. He would guide Clark through physical therapy and become his fantasy football advisor in the fall. He would become Clark's favorite doctor to visit.

With the broken bone addressed, Clark's heart rate and temperature both started to stay in the normal range. Our days in the PICU were numbered. After nineteen days in the unit and a second minor surgery to adjust the pins in his leg, Dr. Pino felt Clark was no longer in need of intensive care and we agreed. It was decided that after lunch he would be moved to the pediatric floor of the hospital.

I would not be honest if I didn't say it scared us to make the move. The staff of the PICU had become like a second family to us. We knew them all by name and we leaned so heavily on Dr. Pino's presence each day. We knew from Debbie's twenty-three years as a nurse that it would be impossible to have the same level of care on the pediatric unit. But our goal was to move forward and leaving the PICU was necessary in order to accomplish it.

This third week had also brought about some drastic changes to our family schedule. Debbie had returned to work and was now shuffling back and forth from work to the hospital and then to home. We could not have survived the pace if my church had not instructed me to stay with Clark. Because of their love for us, I was able to pretty much live at the hospital for the third week. The staff on the pediatric floor was more than happy for me to spend the nights in the room with him and help with his care.

In the evenings I would take a short break and run either back to the motel or home to clean up while Debbie stayed with him. Evenings were now becoming a time when lots of visitors would stop by to see Clark since visiting rules were less restrictive. Almost daily his other "brothers" would stop by. Paul and Brandon had been there for us when we needed them and now they were going to be there for Clark.

I will always believe God used familiar things to help Clark pull back into contact with the real world. Even before his eyes opened in the PICU, we would talk to him often, pray with him and play some of his favorite music from his mp3 player. Clark played the drums in the church praise band and his favorite song was "Beautiful One". We played it for him or sang it to him every day.

Now that we were in a normal room his friends brought a powerful familiarity that God could use. All of them would come into the room and talk to him as though he was talking back. They would fill him in on details about the end of school and about what was going on at church. Paul and Brandon were his video game partners, so they would talk about new games they had played that week.

Paul decided to come by for a while on the second night we were on the floor. He sat by Clark's bed and started talking to him until he had an idea. The kids would call it a "random" idea, meaning an idea from who knows where! Paul decided he would play tic-tac-toe with Clark. He drew up the grid and talked Clark through the whole thing. Paul would even take Clark's hand and fill in the square with an X or an O. A couple of times he even let Clark hold the pencil but it usually dropped to the bed. It was a great try at connecting.

But it turned out to be even more. After a few games Paul put the pencil back into Clark's left hand (he's a southpaw). Paul told him it was his turn and then turned to say something to us. I heard Debbie say, "Look" and we turned quickly enough to see the pencil rise towards the notepad. In one of the open boxes on the grid, Clark put the tip to the paper and drew a diagonal line. He then moved it to the left and drew another line. We all looked at each other to make sure this was really happening. Drawn on the tic-tac-toe grid was now a perfect X.

# Homecoming

We tried for some time to get Clark to repeat making the X but it was the same as the thumbs up episode. It seemed as if he was able to break through into our world for only a few minutes and then he had to slip back to somewhere else. Still, it gave us more hope to see things still changing from day to day.

We had seen several different doctors from the same practice since we had come to the pediatric floor but hadn't had any discussions with them about the planned course of action. For several days things just settled in to caring for Clark's leg and progressing through a few physical therapy steps. On Friday of the third week the PT department sat him up in a tilt chair for the first time. They had to strap him into the chair to keep him from sliding off the chair and onto the floor. It was the first time he had been out of a hospital bed in three weeks.

On Saturday morning one of the doctors made his rounds. Debbie and I were both there when he came in. He sat down at the foot of the bed and asked us if we had given any thought to what we were going to do. I guess we sort of looked puzzled, so he clarified what he was asking. He wanted to know if we had chosen a "nursing facility" yet.

The only discussions we had taken part in before were the ones with the social worker about a brain injury treatment center. The doctor told us those were not options yet because of Clark's unresponsiveness and because of the external fixator on his leg. None of those facilities would take a patient who required the level of physical care he did, so we needed to think in terms of a nursing home until Clark progressed further physically.

Debbie and I were married when we were nineteen and had just celebrated our twenty-sixth wedding anniversary. We've had a lot of discussions about "life" over the years but this was one we didn't need to have. We both looked at each other and I knew exactly what she was thinking because I was thinking the same thing. Then she voiced it. She asked, "When can we take him home?"

We had spent three weeks stunned by the comments of doctors but I think we turned the tables at that moment. He looked at us with a "You can't be serious" look and said, "I suppose today if we can make the necessary arrangements." Keep in mind it was the Saturday before Memorial Day, so making the necessary arrangements wouldn't be easy.

He said he would write the discharge order and someone from the social work department would be in to talk to us. He asked us if we knew just how hard it was going to be to manage his care at home. We both told him we did and he left the room. We looked at each other and at Clark and started to immediately get excited. We were finally taking our boy home.

Now I want to be quick to say we didn't believe it would be somehow "wrong" to move him to a nursing facility. It just wouldn't have been "right" for us. Many families simply have no choice but to make such a move. They might not have the experience to deal with the patient's needs, the support around them that would be necessary, or they might have other children or family members to care for. We knew none of those barriers would impact our decision.

People have asked me if we felt scared about whether we could handle it when we brought him home. I can only speak for myself. In a word - no. For one thing we are reminded in Philippians 4:13 that "I can do all things through Christ who strengthens me." Secondly, if I were dying in a medical emergency there is nobody I would trust more to try and save my life than my wife. Nobody. I knew there was nothing that Clark needed medically that she couldn't handle.

We had a plan and now all we needed were a few doctors, pharmacies, home health agencies, medical equipment companies and a hospital social work department to work together to pull it off on a Saturday before the holiday. No problem!

Debbie immediately left us at the hospital to go home and gather some help. Most of that help came in the form of Clark's Pappaw. He immediately dropped what he was doing, came to our house and helped Debbie transform Clarks' bedroom into a hospital room. They removed and readjusted the furniture, cleared out space for equipment and directed deliveries for the next four hours. His grandfather even built a temporary ramp over a couple of steps leading to the back of our house.

I stayed with Clark at the hospital and met with the social worker as she arranged everything from an immediate home health care visit to a stack of prescriptions for all that Clark would need. The hospital staff worked so hard to help us get home that day. We knew it would have been much easier on them to discharge him after the holiday and we were so appreciative of their effort.

They arranged for us to be picked up by an ambulance service at around 2PM. The first stop we had to make was a pharmacy close to the hospital to get those prescriptions filled. There are no twenty-four hour pharmacies near our home, so we had to be certain we came through the door with everything we needed.

As we left the pharmacy parking lot, I called Debbie on my cell phone and I could hear the excitement in her voice. The medical supply store had done its job and everything was ready on their end – hospital bed, feeding tube machine, IV poles and lifting equipment. The home health agency had called and were scheduled to come in a few hours to help us get Clark settled in.

As we made the forty minute trip from the hospital to our house, I had some time to reflect on just how far God had brought us in twenty-one days. On that Memorial Day weekend, we could have – no should have – been visiting the grave of our only son. But God had a different plan for Clark's life. He had a plan for a hope and a future. He had a purpose to use this situation for His glory and to declare His works to all those who were watching.

# Be Careful What You Ask For

I had no idea of knowing that when I walked through the door to our home, we would be starting the most challenging six months of our lives. The road we were starting down would shake us to the core in every area of our lives: physically, emotionally, spiritually and financially. All we knew for sure was that we would be able to face whatever was to come together as a family. And that would make all the difference!

When you stop and think about it, our lives are made up of a series of progressive steps or events - goals. That truth had been magnified for us since May 7th. We had been asking God for miracle after miracle on a nearly minute by minute basis. "God, please help the rescue workers get him out of the car", "Lord, please let him make it to the hospital alive", "Father, help his cranial pressure stay within safe limits". I'm sure you get the picture.

Our days had been filled with small goals which dealt with each crisis at hand. As Clark had progressed in small ways, we never dared look beyond the next hour or the next procedure. Now as we settled him into the makeshift hospital room that had once just been known as his bedroom. As our family and friends finally left us alone for the first night, there was an unspoken question that started to rise up in both of our minds. Now what?

It wasn't a question that caused any fear or panic. It was just something we hadn't considered before now. Our goals had been simple to this point: get him to the proper medical care, pray he would live, deal with his injuries and get him home. It was all we could see and deal with at the time. But now that the Lord had seen us through all of those goals, we had to consider what the next ones would be.

I meant it with all my heart on the night of the accident when I prayed on the way to the hospital. I told God I didn't care what Clark would be like or what we would have to do to take care of him – I just wanted him to live. So, how would our prayers be answered? Would Clark ever become responsive again? Would he know who we were? Would he ever be able to walk, talk or eat again? Was all this equipment that filled his room going to be temporary or permanent? Believe me, I had asked several doctors those questions and I received the same answer – only time would tell.

As I look back, that point could well have been a major crisis of belief for us if we had been left alone to set those goals ourselves. But we weren't left alone. We had never been alone. We rested in the fact God knew what Clark's future held, even if he hadn't revealed the details to us yet. The fourth man in the car brought healing and help for each step of the journey. Our next steps would be no exception.

Help arrived within hours of coming home. The hospital social worker had contacted a home health agency before we left and their staff was already arriving to assess our situation. They, of course, had only received a verbal description of Clark's condition from the hospital staff. I'm not sure they were prepared for what they actually saw when they stepped into his room that day. In fact, one of the therapists would later tell us the home health team couldn't believe we had chosen to bring Clark home and that she personally believed we had made a terrible mistake.

I've been asked many times to describe exactly what Clark's condition was like when we brought him home. I think the best way I could describe it would be to say that on Memorial Day, 2005, we brought back a corpse with his eyes open. If we had placed him in a casket and closed his eyes, you probably would have complimented the good job the mortician had done. That is until you saw his chest move up and down with every breath!

Let me be a bit more specific. Because of God's protection and miraculous healing, Clark only had two physical problems you could see – the broken femur and the noticeable bruising and swelling caused by the skull fracture and the cut above his left temple. On the outside he looked remarkably normal. The inside, however, was a different story.

The trauma to Clark's brain had left him with no ability to connect with the outside world. He couldn't move at all – not even to help turn himself over. He couldn't swallow and obviously couldn't eat. He couldn't respond to commands or communicate his needs to us in any way.

In that respect we were right back to where we were fifteen years earlier. Every parent knows the frustration of hearing their newborn infant cry and having to guess why they're crying. Are they hungry or tired or, worst of all, are they in pain. Parenting at that stage is pure guesswork. But now we were trying to guess what Clark needed without even the cue of crying to tell us when he had a need. All we could do was stare into eyes and try to get some feel for what he was experiencing.

While Clark was in the hospital, his doctors had kept him on powerful sedation and pain medications to give his brain time to heal and recover. They were also concerned about the pain he might be experiencing from the broken femur. These levels had been so high for so long that we actually brought him home with a care plan normally used to treat drug addicts. His physicians were concerned he might actually go through withdrawal symptoms if we decreased the levels too soon. But by God's grace and care,

Clark seemed to be able to rest without pain which gave us great comfort.

So this is the picture the home health team walked into. It's a wonder they even took the assignment and tried to help us. But help us they did! There were four members of their team – a nurse, a physical therapist, a speech therapist and an occupational therapist. God had placed them in our lives to help us understand what the next steps – those next goals – should be. They individually mapped out specific plans and a specific timetable of their care for Clark. They let us know what they would be doing for our son, and more importantly, what we could do to help him continue to progress.

I know a lot of people were probably saying that we were simply grasping at hope or even a little delusional to keep thinking Clark would ever recover to anywhere approaching normal. But I never doubted the power of God to accomplish his purpose in our son. It didn't make sense to me that God would have performed the series of miracles we had already witnessed, only to bring Clark home to live in a comatose state the rest of his life. God is a God of purpose and I believed from the first day that if He allowed Clark to live it would be for a greater purpose.

# The Gift Of Encouragement

*"God uses a lot of people on the way to a miracle"*
*Debbie Menshouse*

As the Bellefonte Home Health Team began to make their regular visits to our home, we soon got attached to them as part of our family. I actually think it went both ways. Their visits were always an encouragement to us.

Encouragement is becoming a lost art these days. I think part of the reason is we are all so focused on what "we" need or want that we find little time to actually think about the needs of others. And even if we do have a heart that wants to encourage others, we often don't have a clue of how to go about it. We make the mistake of thinking that what we say holds the key to real encouragement but I would disagree. The team members who visited us on a weekly, if not daily, basis encouraged us most by what they "did" for us and by what they shared with us.

On the day that Debbie and her father oversaw the deliveries of all the hospital equipment which would be placed in Clark's room, they also arranged for a twin bed to be moved in. The bed was for me. For the next six months Clark had me as his new roommate. At first it was mandatory because there were things that needed to be done throughout the night to care for him. Later on it served more as a comfort for his Mom and me that I could be with him just to make sure he was OK.

When you are that close to a situation, it's hard to have any real perspective. It's also extremely hard to ever let your mind or body relax. The home health team was able to encourage me in both ways. Their visits, even if for only a few minutes, helped us to step aside and get out from under the pressure of his total care. Debbie had returned to her full time work just before we were able to bring Clark home. She had such a hard balancing act to pull off that I don't know how she did it. She would work her day shift and then come home and spend the rest of her waking day taking care of all the things Clark needed medically.

The team also encouraged us by sharing the changes they could see in Clark from visit to visit. When you're watching things on a day-to-day basis, it's hard to see any progress – especially if that progress is slow. But their perspective was week-to-week and they were able to notice and monitor the healing God was still doing to both his body and his mind.

Two of the team members spent a great deal of time with us and became our greatest encouragers. And to top it all off, they were both Christians who could understand and rejoice in the miracles God was doing in Clark's life. They were his speech therapist, Sonya, and his occupational therapist, Mandy. Sonya and Mandy worked closely together as a team to assess Clark on a week by week basis and formulate a plan of action to move him along. At first their goals were very, very simple. Sonya would focus on developing Clark's ability to swallow while Mandy would attempt to coax some type of cognitive response.

I was quite amazed by their patience as they went about their work. Sonya came each week with her citrus flavored swabs and would gently place them in Clark's mouth to give the sensation of taste. Mandy developed small flash cards which she would hold up in front of Clark which she hoped would provide some type of communication link. At this stage, he was unable to move his body with the exception of slightly moving his left hand. He had attempted a "thumbs up" and made an X on the tic-tac-toe grid in the hospital but those had been the extent of it.

Slowly Clark began to show signs of responding to both Sonya and Mandy. He started to slightly distort his face when Sonya gave him a taste of a swab. It was definitely Clark showing us he didn't particularly like the sour taste that was in his mouth. And after days of repetition, Clark started to slowly lift up his left hand and attempt to point at a card. We couldn't help but laugh, however, when she might ask him, "Is your name Clark?", and watch him point to both "yes" and "no".

It wasn't quite communication but it was a start! Over the next few weeks, Clark's dazed look would begin to vanish and there would be moments of connecting to the world that he had nearly been taken from. It would still come and go but it gave us hope that someday he would be able to communicate with us and tell us what he needed.

Despite only mild victories, our newfound family members pressed on visit after visit. Each time they came into our home you could sense their positive and hopeful outlooks. It energized Debbie and me. It encouraged us. God was indeed using a lot of people on the way to a miracle!

As Clark progressed, there were numerous trips for doctor visits and tests, some by ambulance. It was not only difficult to manage from a logistics viewpoint but it was also becoming increasingly uncomfortable for Clark. He still had the external fixator on his left leg and the transport itself completely wore him out. It was becoming another source of discouragement until one evening we received an email. It was from a pediatrician and friend who attended the church where I pastored. It simply read, "Don't forget - I make house calls." Into our picture of discouragement came Dr. Ann Craig. She was offering the type of encouragement we so desperately needed. She would oversee Clark's care from home!

With the help of Dr. Craig and the Home Health Team, we were squarely back on the path of seeing Clark progress in his recovery. We were being encouraged each day by the actions of others who cared about us and were able to give us some much needed direction. After all, actions speak louder than words, don't they? Not necessarily.

I had returned to a very basic work schedule at the church in late June. Debbie's work schedule allowed me to at least lead our Wednesday evening and Sunday services. The church wasn't requiring me to take those on but I offered to because it helped me as much as it did them. On July 3rd my birthday just happened to be on a Sunday. I went to church that morning and preached at our two morning services.

I got home that day around 1PM with lunch for Debbie. I sat the food down on the table and started towards Clark's room to give them both the Sunday report. As I got near the doorway, I heard Debbie whispering to Clark. I was startled to walk into the room and see my wife with her hands on Clark's chest! It almost looked like she was giving him CPR but the head of his bed was tilted up and he had a grin on his face. As she pushed on his chest three times, I was in the midst of another miraculous moment. "Happy...Birthday...Dad" was the result of those chest pumps. Those were Clark's first words in nearly two months. It was almost too much to take in. We prayed and thanked God for bringing Clark back to us finally. Somebody was home in there. God had given us all the encouraging words we would ever need from the voice of our very own son.

# When I Grow Up

We all grow up wanting to be like somebody. A fireman, a nurse, or a professional athlete would be a few obvious candidates. I think deep down inside every parent hopes they can be a role model for their child. We look up to people who are strong and courageous. We try to emulate people who do great things.

Even though some of my closest friends would question whether I've ever really grown up, I am indeed and adult now. I made my choices and don't have a lot of regrets about them. I'm married to a beautiful and amazing woman and I feel my choice to follow God's call to vocational ministry has given me the opportunity to make a difference in this world. But if I could go back to being a kid, knowing what I know now, there's one person besides Jesus I would want to pattern my life after. That would be my son, Clark.

From the time of the accident until August in 2005, most of what happened was completely out of our control. We were just along for the ride. We were constantly either totally dependent on God's miraculous power or we were leaning on the skills of health professionals. It may sound odd but that was the easy part of Clark's recovery.

Please don't misunderstand what I'm about to say. We are fully aware that there would have been no healing or progress for Clark without God's continued hand upon him. But with that healing came the most demanding part of the long road back, namely his physical recovery. It would be long and hard and would require the most from Clark himself.

During the summer months we had been overjoyed to see Clark's progress in many areas. He was now able to respond, able to speak and able to slowly begin eating. One of the highlights of my summer was watching on a monitor as he passed the swallowing test at a local hospital. But in spite of these motor and cognitive gains, he had made very little progress in his physical therapy.

It wasn't due to a lack of effort on the Home Health team's part. The reality was they were limited in what they could do because of the brain injury and the broken leg. They faithfully came to the house to do range of motion exercises and help him get used to experiencing a sitting position again. But for the most part Clark was totally immobile.

Our normal day consisted of rolling him from side to side multiple times a day to prevent the development of bedsores. At least once a day, I would lift him up to position where he could sit on the side of the bed and I would just hold him there. If I really felt brave, I would give him a bear hug and stand him up on his feet for a few short minutes in the hope he could regain some sense of balance and feel for standing. It wasn't as much a strain on me as it would have been considering Clark had now lost around sixty pounds in just two months. It broke my heart that one of the first few times we stood him up, he passed out on my shoulder.

I would be lying if I said I always had the faith to believe Clark would walk again. To be honest, there were many days I thought he might be bound to either a bed or a wheelchair for the rest of his life. There were days when we became so exhausted from the grind that I started to second guess our decision to bring him home. Were we doing the best thing for him?

But when I would start to doubt, it only took me looking at his face to know he was where he belonged. I will always believe that being at home in such familiar surroundings and having constant contact with his family and friends were key factors in the remarkable progress he made. Yes, it would have been easier on us to have someone else do the lifting and the therapy and the personal care. But for our family it was the right thing. Nobody knew him like we knew him. We could anticipate his needs, we knew what he liked and didn't like and we could surround him with an atmosphere of love and prayer at all times.

So our short-term goal became making his life as "normal" as possible in the hopes that familiar things would trigger improvements. Gradually I was able to turn the moments of sitting up on the side of the bed to short stints in a recliner. At first they were dead lifts to stand Clark up and carry him to the chair. Soon, however, I could feel him attempting to balance his own weight. He even progressed to being able to put his arms around my neck and hold on ever so gently.

At the point where Clark could sit in a chair for few minutes, his friends started to come over regularly and get in on the action. His friend Paul, who he made the "X" for in the hospital, would come and sit by Clark and play video games while Clark looked on. I mentioned Clark fit into the "gamer" social class at school and playing video games with Paul was one of his favorite things to do. Paul was such a good friend that he even came up with the idea he would help Clark hold the video game controller and would move his fingers to press the buttons! It was Paul's way of trying to rescue his buddy who was still trapped inside that body. And it worked.

With every hour he sat in a chair, with every ride he took in the car and with every trip we made outside in his wheelchair, Clark's body was slowly responding and progressing. By the middle of August, the physical therapist, who had been making the home visits, decided he had done all that he could do for us in the home. The time had come to see just how far Clark could progress physically. In order to accomplish that, we would need to begin outpatient physical therapy at the local hospital.

The call was made to set up the initial assessment and we were scheduled to be seen at the beginning of the following week. I was both excited and scared. I was excited about the fact the therapist had seen enough progress to warrant this next step. But I was scared about what the future would hold. Just how far back could he come? I thought, "What if the prognosis is that we've seen as much progress as we'll ever see?" I was actually worried about all the wrong things. What I should have been worried about was how I would be able to keep up with where God was going to take Clark in the next six months!

I'm sure we must not have been what they were expecting when we rolled through the door that first morning (and I do mean rolled). Clark had to travel in an extra wide wheelchair because of the external fixator in his leg, so we entered the lobby in our "double-wide" and asked who we were to see. The receptionist introduced us to one of the physical therapists who would do our initial assessment and she led the way to an exam room. By now Clark and I had established somewhat of a routine to get in and out of the wheelchair. He still couldn't stand on his own but at least he could help me help him. I lifted him onto the exam table and turned to ask the therapist if he was where she wanted him to be. There was a look of shock on her face. She didn't say it but I knew what she was thinking. Who made the judgment call that this kid was ready for outpatient therapy? He could barely move, so what exactly were they supposed to do for him?

She politely worked with us to fill out the information sheet, including the history of how we got to this point. She checked Clark out from head to toe and then began to explain how the process would work. We were to come back on Wednesday and begin a two visit per week regiment. The first few visits would be focused on assessment and then they would present us with a care plan and the outcome they felt we could expect from physical therapy. It was a start but the hesitation I could sense only caused me to question where all of this was headed. Since Clark was exhausted from the visit, we returned home and got him settled for a long nap. That would become our schedule for the rest of the year – therapy followed by a nap!

If we had learned anything to this point, we had learned that the Lord was watching over Clark at every step of the journey. From the moment the car struck the pole, God had been with us and had given us the strength we needed for each day. It's so easy for us to get caught up in the moment that we forget God is also providing for our future. He's always one step ahead of us in his care for us. Now, at the most grueling time in his recovery, God had already chosen someone to guide us the rest of the way.

When we returned on Wednesday to begin Clark's physical therapy, we were supposed to see the same therapist but, for some unexplained reason, we had been assigned to someone else. One of the therapists pointed in the distance to a young lady with short brown hair and identified her as the person who would guide Clark's physical rehabilitation.

She was finishing up with another patient, so I rolled Clark's wheelchair around the walking track towards her station. After just a few short minutes we were greeted by the one person who would impact Clark's recovery the most. Her name was Donna.

I believe God placed Donna in Clark's life because she was everything he needed at that point. She was calm, confident, positive, compassionate and had a sense of humor. Clark needed all those things for the tough road ahead of him. I believe God chose her because she had the ability to draw out the best in him.

That process of drawing out the best began almost immediately. She had read his chart and had already laid out some plans to increase his flexibility and muscle tone. She put him to work on the spot. I was amazed at Donna's reaction (or lack of reaction) to Clark. She didn't seem the least bit intimidated that her new patient was a sixteen year old kid who could barely move or talk and who had a TV antenna sticking out of the side of his leg! She guided him up onto a padded therapy table and began to help him stretch and exercise in ways we were not able to at home.

As Clark and Donna became a team, I started to see a side of Clark I had not seen before. Before the accident he was very quiet and timid. Nothing ever seemed to worry him and nothing ever seemed to really capture his total focus and energy. Now, as he returned day after day to the Vitality Center, I was starting to see a determination that was brand new. He was determined to try and do whatever Donna asked him to do and he was going to keep trying until he succeeded. If she gave him exercises to do at home, then he would do those two or three times. If she challenged him to lift a weight a certain number of times, then he would always try for one extra repetition.

His determination even led to a nickname from Donna – "GRRR". It was the sound he made when he was straining to get those last reps in or complete the last lap. She would growl at him as a reminder to push hard to the finish. He would grin and growl back until he reached his goal. During his time in rehab, Clark spent two weeks back in the hospital with a ruptured appendix, which was in itself life-threatening. Donna visited him in the hospital and brought a gift – a little tiger with the nametag "GRRR". The name fit perfectly.

What started out as a program of stretches and small arm weights gradually became activities to help with balance and core body control. Donna helped him learn to sit and stand on his own with the help of a walker and then gradually to put one foot in front of the other. As the pins came out of Clark's leg, Donna added weight training and agility drills.

With God's healing power and Donna's skill and encouragement, the same boy I lifted up on the examination table in August was running around the track in January! How could that be? In my wildest imagination I would have pictured Clark perhaps walking in a year or two. But right before my eyes God was reminding me of Ephesians 3:20-21, *"Now to Him who is able to do exceedingly abundantly above all that we ask or think, according to the power that works in us, to Him be glory in the church by Christ Jesus to all generations, forever and ever. Amen."* (NKJV)

God had used Donna to change Clark's life forever and she would later tell us it went both ways. When God brought the two of them together, Donna was becoming discouraged and burned out as a therapist. She often wondered if what she was doing was ever really making a lasting difference. Clark answered that question for her. Isn't it amazing that when we make ourselves available to God to serve others, we receive what we need from God?

Who do I want to be like when I grow up? I would like to be more like my son who never gave up hope; who never quit when it hurt too much; who never complained about what he was going through. I would like to have a little more of his discipline and gratitude. I wouldn't trade him for anyone in the world, scars and all.

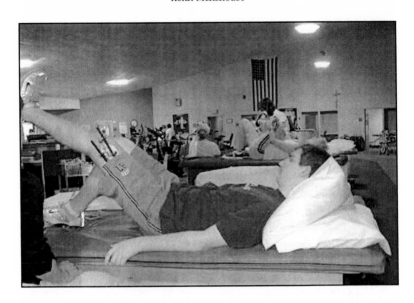

# The Rest Of The Story

*'...for this my son was dead and is alive again; he was lost and is found.' And they began to be merry.*
*Luke 15:24 (NKJV)*

God certainly does use a lot of people on the way to a miracle. God performs some miracles instantly. He chose to give us our miracle slowly.

Albert Einstein may be most famous for his theory of relativity which is often talked about when the topic of time travel comes up. Time is truly relative, isn't it? We gauge its passage relative to what we are currently experiencing. If we're enjoying ourselves, then time seems to pass quickly. We often say that, "Time flies when you're having fun!" But when we are going through difficulty, we describe time as "standing still" or "dragging by". It's all relative.

As we traveled through the darkest time in our lives, it truly seemed it would never end. Every day was so overwhelming we couldn't let ourselves look beyond the task that was at hand – the next medication, the next therapy session or the next dressing change. There were lots of mornings we awoke with just one prayer – "Lord, please help us just make it through this day".

Lots of people have asked us how we were able to cope with the pressure. How did it not destroy us as a couple? How were we able to keep going and not give up or quit? I hope you're beginning to see the answer to that question. As dark as it seemed all around us, we were experiencing a supernatural miracle from the Maker of the universe! He was not only doing things for us but, most importantly, he was with us through our long night. We were learning what King David meant in the 23rd Psalm when he wrote, *"Yea, though I walk through the valley of the shadow of death, I will fear no evil; For You are with me; Your rod and Your staff, they comfort me." (NKJV)*

God's comfort came to us in many ways. He gave us rainbows. He prompted phone calls. He led people to send cards and share verses. But one thing that served as a vehicle for God's comfort the most was music. I can't tell you how many times Debbie and I would be so down and discouraged only to get into our car and hear God speak comfort to us through the words of a song.

Most often, the Lord used the music of the group Casting Crowns to heal us to the point where we could go on another day. I look forward to someday in Heaven when I will be able to sit down with them and thank them for their faithful ministry. Their song, *The Voice Of Truth*, gave us the strength we needed to face each day in the intensive care unit. Each time we would get a negative report from a CT scan or hear that Clark's condition had become more critical, we would sing the chorus in our hearts that *"The Voice of Truth tells me a different story, the Voice of Truth says 'do not be afraid' and the Voice of Truth says this is for my glory! Out of all the voices calling out to me, I will choose to listen and believe the Voice of Truth"* I'm afraid that if it hadn't been for that song then we would have listened to the other voices around us and missed God's comforting voice.

God also used our church family to hold us up when we couldn't stand on our own. At the time of the accident, I had nearly completed my sixth year as pastor of the Oakland Avenue Baptist Church in Catlettsburg, Kentucky. In six short years we had already been through a great deal together as a church family.

Debbie and I had both lost parents during that time and the church had been grieving for several key leaders who had gone home to be with the Lord. We were in the midst of completing long range planning and a major renovation project at the time of the wreck.

They reached out to us in many ways, the most important one being prayer. During the first few days in intensive care, someone from our church was praying for Clark around the clock. Literally twenty-four hours a day! They communicated specific prayer needs to people and churches all across our region. There were dozens of calls to the church office asking what they could do to help us, but there were two things the church did for us for which I will forever be grateful.

The first one was the toughest. They left us alone. Does that sound strange to you? If so, then let me explain. From the very first few hours after the wreck, it became clear that our undivided attention had to be focused on Clark. It wasn't only that we "needed" to be with him every minute, but we "wanted" to be with him and spend as much time with him as would be allowed by the hospital staff.

I remember walking out into the emergency waiting room on the first night and wondering how I could handle communicating with so many people. They each were there because they cared about us and wanted to help, but every minute I spent talking with them, bringing them up to speed with the latest report, was another minute I could not be at Clark's side. So I sent word to my secretary that we would request no visitors at the hospital. They loved us enough to honor our wishes.

I didn't realize what a burden I had placed on them until about a year later. My secretary, Diane, had given me a log she had kept while Clark was in the hospital. She recorded every call which came in to the church and everyone who stopped by the office to offer their help. There were dozens. People mailed cards and sent snacks to the nursing staff and dropped off coins for the vending machines. They were straining to find some way to let us know they loved us. But I often wonder if they realized they gave us what we needed the most – time to be alone with our son!

The second thing they did for us was unexpected and made such a difference in Clark's rehabilitation. They wouldn't let me go. One of the first messages I received from our deacons following the accident was to not worry about things at the church and to take as much time off as I needed. We had a very capable staff and they jumped right in to take care of the daily operations and weekend services.

It took several weeks to get Clark settled in at home but by late June I attempted a return to pastoring. All I could manage was to lead the four services we held each week and to attend a few important meetings. It didn't take long to realize I couldn't be in two places at one time, either physically or emotionally. I couldn't focus on the needs of the congregation. Every minute I was in the office, I spent more time wondering about Clark's condition than accomplishing anything for Oakland Avenue Baptist Church. I started to feel it wasn't fair to the church family to leave them without a shepherd indefinitely. So on Labor Day weekend, I announced to the church I would be resigning immediately to devote my time to Clark's rehabilitation.

That evening the church leadership met to discuss my announcement. After the meeting I received a phone call informing me they were not going to receive my resignation. They asked me instead to take a leave of absence through the remainder of the calendar year. They wanted me to spend that time with Clark and then re-evaluate the situation before making a final decision. It would give us time to see how Clark progressed and to pray about the future. But that wasn't the entire offer. They told me they were going to continue to pay my full salary and benefits. They didn't want us to worry about finances. They only wanted us to focus on our son.

At the end of the year I still was not able to return to a full-time pastorate. Even though Clark had come such a long way, there were multiple therapy and doctor visits each week as well as tutoring to try and finish high school. To be honest, at that point in time I did not see myself ever pastoring again. But God had used his people, the church, to serve and protect us in our greatest time of need and our family will forever be grateful to them for their graciousness and love.

The message of music and the love of a church family were two of the many ways God helped us walk day after day down our long, dark tunnel. But as the song by Third Day reminds us, "There's a light at the end of this tunnel for me". I now have the luxury of viewing our experience in that light and seeing it as a whole. I am in awe of who God is and what he has done. I feel like Moses when he said, *"O Lord GOD, You have begun to show Your servant Your greatness and Your mighty hand, for what god is there in heaven or on earth who can do anything like Your works and Your mighty deeds?" (Deuteronomy 3:24 NKJV)*

It has now been just over five years since that phone call on May 7, 2005 and while the whole story will continue to be written by Clark's life, I am honored to recount what God has done to this point. We have leaned on Psalm 117:18: *"I shall not die, but live, and declare the works of the Lord."* God kept his part of the promise and now we are attempting to keep ours.

To put it all in perspective, I developed the following timeline:

**May 7** – The accident. He is trapped in his car for nearly two hours.

**May 8** – Admitted to PICU with broken femur, basilar skull fracture and severe traumatic brain injury. The doctor described the CT scan as "the worst head bleed" she had ever seen.

**May 23** – Transferred home with no mobility, on a feeding tube and still unresponsive. A Home Health Team oversees his care.

**July 3** – Speaks for the first time.

**First week of August** – Begins physical therapy in a wheelchair.

**Mid-August** – Passes a swallowing test and begins to supplement feeding tube with liquids and soft foods.

**First of September** – Surgery is performed to remove pins from his femur. He is fitted with a leg brace.

**September 14** (his birthday) – Hospitalized with a ruptured appendix. Two surgeries are required and Clark spends two weeks in the hospital.

**September 30** – Hospitalized again do to an incorrect placement of a new feeding tube. Another surgery is required and Clark returns home without a feeding tube. He begins to eat on his own.

**Mid-October** – Begins walking with the help of a walker.

**Mid-November** – The walker is no longer needed.

**Mid-January** – Discharged from physical therapy. Clark is now able to run short distances. He starts workouts at the local YMCA three days per week.

**May 2006** – Graduates with high school class after completing Senior English class at home.

**August 2006** – Enrolls at Ashland Community and Technical College.

As I look back over the timeline, it reminds me of just who God is. He is the God who can do anything! He is the God who says, *"I'll turn conventional wisdom on its head"* (1 Corinthians 1:19 The Message). He is the God who loves us and watches over us and whose heart is broken when we are broken. He is the God of miracles.

As I write this book, Clark is a junior at Western Kentucky University majoring in Computer Information Technology and carries a GPA above three. His only lasting physical problem is an unnoticeable slight weakness on his right side. From a cognitive perspective he has two lasting effects: a lack of short term memory and a difficulty in forming sentences in his mind before he speaks. If you were to talk with him, you might notice he will begin a sentence and then rephrase it before he finishes his point.

If you met him on the street or in the mall, I'm confident you would never notice anything different. But things are definitely different! The physical limitations will probably always be with him, and that's alright. He's learned to adjust and adapt. The major differences, however, are on the inside and that in itself is a miracle.

As a sixteen year-old pastor's kid, I could see Clark starting to struggle with his faith. He was starting to pull away from church and family like most adolescents in a search for identity and values. We spent a lot of time together but talked less and less about important things. The traditional church model was becoming less appealing to him and I think he would tell you he had relegated his relationship with God to a back burner. There's no way to know for sure but my best guess is he would have gone off to college and really questioned his faith and wrestled with his choices.

I don't know where he would be today if nothing had ever happened but I certainly know where he is now. The post-accident Clark is a young man who is fully aware the Lord miraculously spared his life. And because of his experience, as he would put it, of "being with God" for the months following the accident, his faith puts his parents' faith to shame. He has developed one of the most "real" relationships with God I have ever seen.

What's amazing is that not only do I see the change that has happened in his life but he sees it too. And what's even more amazing is he is glad the changes have come. In fact, he's at peace with how they have come. One day, not too long ago, we were standing in our kitchen at home. We had been talking about what the last five years had been like for us as a family. Clark looked at us and said, "I know this will sound terrible, but I'm sort of glad the wreck happened."

His mother reminded him that he couldn't remember the first three months. But we both knew what he meant. He might not remember the accident but he remembers what his faith was like before it all happened. Now his faith is real and personal and he wouldn't trade it for anything he had to go through. It took a near death to bring him to life.

# Why Me?

I know what you're probably thinking. You've been bracing yourself all along for the part where we start feeling sorry for ourselves and wonder what we ever did to deserve this. Am I right? Well, before you order the cake, put up the decorations, and send out the invitations to our Pity Party, just hold on for a second and hear me out.

I'm sure it wouldn't surprise you to know I'm not the only person, or the only pastor, to ever ask the question, "Why me?" It seems to be a common occurrence for anyone who has experienced a loss or a tragedy in their lives. Our churches are filled every Sunday with hurting people who are asking that very question. But nobody seems to be talking it. Instead of searching for answers from Scripture, we feel more comfortable making vague references to the "mysteries" of God's will or shaming people for even asking the question in the first place.

Since the time I was a teenager, I have been convinced God gave us a mind to think with. One of my favorite verses in the Bible is Isaiah 1:18, where God invites us to *"Come now, and let us reason together," Says the Lord, "Though your sins are like scarlet, they shall be as white as snow; though they are red like crimson, they shall be as wool."* (NKJV) Or as the New Living Translation reads, *"Come now, let's settle this, says the Lord.*" I'm afraid there are many of us who have stopped growing in our relationship to God because of something we never "settled" in the past. Perhaps you need to know where God was in the middle of your personal tragedy. Maybe you struggle with what the purpose of your suffering was or what lesson you were supposed to learn. Some of us have even posed the most paralyzing question of what did we do that angered God to the point He would cause such suffering. Why me?

I don't believe the problem is that we are asking questions. When I was in high school I had the life-changing opportunity to hear Josh McDowell, a well-known Christian scholar and apologist, speak at a college campus near my home. I had never heard anyone speak with such confidence about his faith. He had become a Christian while attempting to disprove the claims of Jesus from the Bible. He later wrote a book entitled *Evidence That Demands A Verdict*. It's basically the Encyclopedia Britannica on subjects like the trustworthiness of the Bible, the historical truth of the resurrection and many other topics. I read every word of it. And in doing so, I discovered God was not only "OK" with my honest questions but He actually wanted me to think and reason out my faith. That's why he revealed Himself to us in the Bible and in His Son, Jesus.

So if the problem is not asking questions, what is it? I think it's in asking the wrong questions. By "wrong" I don't mean evil or against the rules. What I mean is we often ask questions which don't really lead us to the truths we need to "settle it". Now in all honesty, we get many of those wrong questions from our experiences with other believers who mean well but have never searched the Scriptures for their own beliefs.

Let me share an example with you. I was standing in the hallway of a church I pastored on a Sunday morning. I saw the door open and in walked a young lady whose infant child had just died weeks before. Several of the women in the hallway rushed to greet her and they each gave her a hug to comfort her. Then

I heard one of the women offer these words of encouragement. She said, "I'm so sorry for your loss. I guess God needed another little angel in Heaven more than you needed her here on Earth." Really? I was stunned. I waited for somebody to correct her or offer some other explanation for the woman's suffering. But instead, they all chimed in with "That's right" or "We just can't understand these things right now". So off to the sanctuary they scurried to worship a god who kills babies just for the joy of having another soul to serve him.

It's no wonder George Barna recently surveyed people across our state and found that 80% of those who do not attend church *used* to attend church. He identified several key factors, one of them being an attitude of judgmentalism. But the one reason which stood out to me the most was that the church had become "irrelevant" in their lives. That's what happens when you give hurting people answers to their questions that come more from the movie *It's A Wonderful Life* than from the Bible! We can't become lazy and flippant with answers to the questions which matter most.

So let's ask those questions that are on our hearts but never make it past our lips. But before I begin to share the answers I've arrived at in my own faith journey, let me make a disclaimer. These are deep questions which could, and in many cases already have, fill up entire books. My purpose here is not to cover every aspect of the discussion. My purpose is simply to share some building blocks to help you on your way.

Let's start with, "Why me?" That may be how we phrase the question, but the real issue at hand Is, "What did I do to cause my suffering?" That's fair enough. It's been asked for centuries, not only by the people who are going through trying times but also by those who are watching from the outside. In the Gospel of John, chapter nine, Jesus and his disciples were walking by a blind man. The question on the disciples' minds was this: *"Rabbi, who sinned: this man or his parents, causing him to be born blind?"*

One of the most hurtful things we had to endure in our situation was to hear people's insinuations that something must be spiritually wrong in our lives in order for this to happen to us. Things must not be as they appear at the pastor's house. There must be some "sin in the camp" God was punishing us for. That type of thinking is what captured the minds of the disciples. It easily captures ours.

So why do bad things happen in our lives? Let me break the answer down into three possibilities:

1.  You and I can be the direct cause of what's happening to us.

It's true in a couple of ways. First of all, our actions almost always have consequences. That was true for Clark. We can take all the mystery out of the "why" in our situation by agreeing that if Clark had chosen not to race, then there wouldn't have been a car wreck. The pole didn't slam into the car. It was the other way around.

Secondly, sometimes our wrong choices bring discipline from our Heavenly Father. The Bible says in Hebrews 12:6 that, "The Lord disciplines those he loves, and he punishes everyone he accepts as his child." (NCV) You discipline your children, don't you? Why? You do it because you love them. You want them to be safe and to learn right from wrong. God loves us even more than we do our own children and wants those things for us. How do we go about correcting our children? We use the mildest form of punishment we think will produce the desired result. Our Heavenly Father will do no less. He will only allow what is needed to help us change our course.

Let me add one other thought before we move on. I've never disciplined Clark and then said, "Now guess what you did wrong?" I've never punished him for something he did months or years earlier. The punishment always comes swiftly and I tell him why he's being punished. To discipline him in any other way would create fear and bitterness between us instead of a change in behavior. If you're experiencing a crisis and you don't know what you did wrong or when you did it, maybe you need to continue to search for another reason and stop blaming God.

2.  We can be the target of a spiritual attack.

If you are a follower of Jesus then you have an enemy. The Bible calls him Satan. 1 Peter 5:8 cautions us to, *"Stay alert! Watch out for your great enemy, the devil. He prowls around like a roaring lion, looking for someone to devour."* *(NLT)* I'm bringing up the possibility of what has been called Spiritual Warfare because I do believe it is a biblical concept but not nearly as prevalent as some would have us believe.

There are rare occasions when God allows Satan to "test" our faith. In the Old Testament, Satan approached God and asked permission to test the faith of Job. In the New Testament, Jesus warns Peter that Satan had asked permission to "sift" him like wheat. In both of these cases we are reminded Satan does not have unlimited power over us to do whatever he would like. God only allows Satan's attacks to come in a controlled manner and God's promise is He will be with us to insure our faith does not fail. The Bible pictures these attacks as being mostly directed at leaders in the Church and for specific purposes. I would caution you that while every trial in our life has a spiritual impact on us (Romans 8:28, Ephesians 6:12), they are not all the result of direct Satanic attacks.

3.  We live in a fallen world.

Before I discuss the most important way of looking at an explanation, let me tell you a story about Clark when he was about 6 years old. At the end of kindergarten, Clark was diagnosed with type 1 diabetes. He was hospitalized for a few days and we immediately had to start the regiment of multiple insulin injections per day. He's worn an insulin pump since the age of nine.

We had a wonderful pediatric endocrinologist who tried to communicate very clearly that Clark's condition was hereditary and there was nothing anyone had done to "cause" it. But before such a truth could sink into his young heart, a social worker at the hospital made the comment to him that, "Only special little angels get diabetes". I know she meant well, but she only reinforced what he was already thinking. Bad things only happen to people who do bad things!

So one evening after coming home from the hospital, Clark strolled into our small barn where Debbie was feeding our rabbits. While I was in seminary in North Carolina, she took up the hobby of raising rabbits to show in the state fair and other competitions. He looked up at her and asked, "Momma, if I do something else bad, will I get another disease?" Wow! Talk about out of the mouth of babes.

I wasn't there for the conversation which followed, but I didn't need to be. Momma was the one Clark needed to hear it from. She will tell you she doesn't know how the words came out of her mouth, but she told our son exactly what I'm going to tell you now. She said, "No, no, Honey. God's crying with you and hates it too." She then explained a spiritual truth which every 6 year old who has grown up in church can understand but we grown-ups have forgotten.

She simply started at the start! *"In the beginning God created the heavens and the earth"*- Genesis 1:1 (NKJV). Just about every Sunday School class and Vacation Bible School Clark had ever attended taught him this basic truth. God created the universe we live in. He wanted it to be the perfect home for Adam and Eve and all their descendants. The Bible even adds that on the final day of creation, *"God saw everything that He had made, and indeed it was very good."*

What did God make? He made a "perfect" universe. He constructed a perfect garden and placed the first man and woman in an environment which was designed as their home forever. You heard me right. The Bible records there was even a tree in the garden called the Tree of Life. It had the ability to sustain Adam and Even physically. It was never God's intention that they ever die.

But we know what was to follow. God placed them in their new home with only one restriction. Genesis 2: 16-17 records God's warning: *"You may eat the fruit from any tree in the garden, but you must not eat the fruit from the tree which gives the knowledge of good and evil. If you ever eat fruit from that tree, you will die!"* (NCV) Adam and Eve both chose to disobey God and the very moment they did, they brought death into God's perfect world.

Before their sin in the garden, there was no mechanism for death or suffering. There were no diseases. There were no natural disasters. There was no crime or violence or even a threat from the animals surrounding them. But after their sin, the whole world changed. The Bible describes the whole universe as coming under the "curse" of Adam and Eve's sin. God created everything perfectly and we destroyed it by our own choices. But that's not the end of the story!

God will someday make a new Heaven and Earth. It will be perfect just like the first one with on huge exception. There will be no danger of destroying it ever again. Because Jesus died on the Cross to pay the penalty of our sin, we are invited to place our trust in Him. By our act of simple faith, we will live eternally in a place described as a home where, *"God himself will be with them. He will wipe every tear from their eyes, and there will be no more death or sorrow or crying or pain."* - Revelation 21:3-4 (NLT)

In our small wooden barn, Clark listened to every word his Momma said that day. She concluded her rabbit barn sermon by saying, "You didn't do anything wrong to get diabetes. We just live in a world that is broken and has diseases right now. Someday God is going to fix it all and we won't have diabetes or anything else bad." In the total honesty of a trusting child, he looked up at her and said, "Oh. OK". He left the barn with a smile on his face and a peace in his heart.

How about you? Do you have any peace? Are you still wondering why God has caused some tragedy in your life? Are you still wondering what you did to deserve it? If so, let me take you back to the passage we read earlier involving Jesus, the disciples and the blind man. Jesus' response to their question of guilt was simple. He looked at them and said, *"You're asking the wrong question. You're looking for someone to blame. There is no such cause-effect here. Look instead for what God can do."* - John 9:3 – (MSG)

It's time for me to answer the question. Did I ever ask God, "Why me?" Yes. I asked it dozens of times, but not in the way we've been discussing it to this point. I never blamed God for what happened that night. The truth, as hard as it was to accept, was that Clark had made a terrible mistake in judgment and it set in motion the consequences which should have ended his life that night. He made a mistake and was paying the ultimate price for it. I knew God loved us and was wrapping his arms of comfort around us every moment. He wasn't the enemy. He was our friend and our comforter.

Clark and I have had many opportunities to share our story with high schools and church youth groups over the past few years. Almost without exception, someone will come up to us and share that a brother or sister or child was killed in an automobile accident. The look on their face always leaves me with a sense of confusion and, to be frank, a feeling of guilt. What I really hear them saying is they are glad it all worked out for us but what about them? Where was their miracle?

So, what I find myself asking is, "God, why me? Why did you choose to do this miracle in my family? Why did you keep my son alive? Why me?" I'm still working through the right answer to those questions but I can already tell you what some wrong ones are.

God didn't spare Clark's life because of the faith of his Mom and Dad. There were many times throughout the past five years that we didn't have much faith at all. He also didn't intervene as a payback for devoting my life to ministry. I get a little weary of hearing people quote 3 John 2 as if it were some investment formula. It says, *"Beloved, I pray that you may prosper in all things and be in health, just as your soul prospers."* (NKJV) This text is abused in the churches of our day to say God's will for everyone who follows Him is to be healthy and wealthy – no exceptions! I can't wait to hear what the Apostles, who all died martyrs deaths, have to say about that when we get to Heaven.

So why did God provide a miracle for Clark? All I can do is once again listen to Jesus' explanation to his disciples. *"Look instead for what God can do."* God does the miraculous when He has a purpose to fulfill through that miracle. God had a reason – a purpose – for protecting and restoring Clark. I know that sounds like another vague, spiritual answer but please, hear me out.

Even if you have been open to the reasons I have laid out for tragedy in our lives, you probably have one final question. Couldn't God have prevented what happened to me? The answer, in a word, is "Yes". He is the sovereign, all-powerful and all-knowing Creator. But the question isn't "Could he?" The real question is "Why would he?" prevent it. Why would God suspend the laws of nature (as they are now) and prevent what's going to happen?

Did I hear you say, "He would do it if He loved me"? Please think that statement through to its logical conclusion. If God loves someone then he prevents all tragedy, sickness and death from occurring. According to John 3:16, God loves the whole world. Then God should prevent all tragedy, sickness and death from happening. Period. Isn't that what we're really saying? Yet we don't really expect Him to prevent everything negative, do we? That's not going to be the reality of this world, but it will be the reality of Heaven someday. It's why Jesus died for us. He gave his life because he loves us so much that he wants us to be in Heaven with him forever.

I had to face my bias about God's love in 1993 when my father died. Clark was only five years old. My dad was the best dad anyone could ever hope for. We shared a lot of things together but none more than our love of sports. Actually, I probably just had his love of sports passed down. He was at every ballgame I ever played in and we would spend time together watching any type of sporting event that came on TV. Our favorite thing to do was watch the University of Kentucky Wildcat basketball team (sort of a birthright if you're born in the Bluegrass State). From the moment Clark was born, I couldn't wait for my Dad to start to rub off on him. When Clark was a baby, they would sit in the floor for hours and play.

Then one day, my Dad started to have back soreness. In 53 days he was dead from cancer. It was one of the toughest times in my life. The last thing we ever did together was watch UK in the NCAA tournament from his hospital room. I was in seminary at the time, so I was driving from Kentucky to North Carolina just after the funeral. I remember wearing God out! Why me? Why now? Couldn't he have healed my Dad so Clark could grow up knowing him? He'll never remember my Dad. Couldn't this have waited until Clark was out of school and had Pappaw in the stands for his games? It went on and on. I'm so thankful God lets us yell at him even when he is not a fault.

Somewhere on the road home that day, I guess a light went on. I wasn't really asking God to give me a few more years with my Dad. If God had said, "Okay. I'll heal him now and he'll die after Clark graduates", would I have been fine with that? No. I would have wanted my Dad to see Clark get his first job. I would have wanted my Dad at Clark's wedding and to hold and play with Clark's children. I finally had to ask myself the question of when would I be alright with Dad dying? The truthful answer was never. So I was able that day to let go of my Dad and to stop accusing God of not loving me anymore. I realized I had no right to ask God for a miracle that did not have a purpose.

Only time will tell what the purpose was for the miracle in our home. Perhaps it is as simple as you having an opportunity to read this book and understand God is your friend and not your enemy. He is with you through whatever is happening to you and will never leave you. He didn't cause it or send it upon you. He hurts with you and has prepared a place for you where you'll never again have to ask the question, "Why Me?"

# Woulda, Coulda, Shoulda

*My friend had a vineyard on a hill with very rich soil. He dug
and cleared the field of stones and planted the best grapevines
there. He built a tower in the middle of it and cut out a winepress
as well. He hoped good grapes would grow there, but only bad
ones grew. My friend says, "You people living in Jerusalem, and
you people of Judah, judge between me and my vineyard. What
more could I have done for my vineyard than I have already done?*
Isaiah 5:1-4 (NCV)*

When I was a young pastor serving in the Cleveland area, a friend
and I traveled over to Hammond, Indiana to attend a pastor's
conference. There I heard the late Jack Hyles preach a sermon
based on this passage from the book of Isaiah. I have been drawn
to the question in the last verse ever since. What more could I
have done in my vineyard than I have already done?

Some of us might take that question to mean the owner of
the vineyard was second guessing himself. Have you ever gone
down that road? What if I would have …If I could only have…I
should have…. You can drive yourself crazy playing the Woulda,
Shoulda, Coulda game. It only leaves you with a bunch of regrets
you probably can't do anything about.

What more could I have done in my marriage? What more
could I have done to take care of my parents? What more could

I have done to keep my job? Those regrets can easily capture you in a prison of guilt if you're not careful. It's definitely a place God doesn't want you to be.

I don't believe, however, the grape farmer is taking a trip down memory lane. I don't see his question as a look back at his failures. I see it as a rhetorical question with the answer of "nothing". Now granted, things hadn't worked out in the vineyard the way he had planned. The vines weren't producing good grapes but it was not for lack of effort on his part. He had done all he could have done to make it a success and he has a sense of peace within himself. Is it possible to have a peace in your life about your past? I believe so – correction, I know so.

There were lots of negative effects on all of our lives from Clark's accident. I've talked at length about how his life has been changed by it. The same is true, however, for his mother and me. There's hardly anything we do that doesn't directly affect someone else. Our credit was destroyed after finally leaving the church and living on one income for some time. Debbie still can't relax when Clark's out at night, even if he's with people we know we can trust. The sight of a yellow car immediately brings back memories of her picking paint chips for days from his hair. But there was one thing which grew out of reflecting on the accident, all the money in the world couldn't buy. It was a peace from having no regrets.

I preached my first sermon at the age of fourteen and started serving part-time on a church staff at age sixteen. Starting in the ministry at such an early age gave me lots of opportunities to travel around the area (alright, be driven by my Mom and Dad!) to speak to church youth groups. I became more and more involved in leading youth projects on an area-wide scale. That, in turn, translated into spending lots of time around pastors and their families.

It didn't take me long to question most of what I saw. I don't intend for this to sound like a blanket indictment of all pastors. Some of them had great relationships with their kids. But sadly, most did not. What I started to hear from many of the pastor's children was that their Dad was never around and had no idea about what was going on in their lives. Most of them were convinced their fathers didn't care half as much about them as they did their church members. And the pastors only reinforced that feeling by choosing meetings over ballgames and spending most evenings away from home.

As I've grown older, I have observed this as a problem for men in general. We choose to link our identity to our work. We strive to be known for what we do or what we have instead of for who we are. In fact, most of us don't want anyone to know who we really are – including our families.

The trap of sacrificing his family for his church is a constant danger for a pastor. In a sad way, lots of pastors see the choice of church over family as a sign of their own superior spirituality. I've heard some say, "If I want to reach people for Christ then I have to be willing to make whatever sacrifice is necessary?" Really? Please tell me you don't mean that. If it's truly what you think, then stay single and don't have children!

As a result of my experiences, I started to form some strong opinions about priorities in our lives. As Debbie and I started to date, we talked often about what a life in ministry would be like and what Biblical priorities would look like. So, from the time I started serving in my first pastorate in Cleveland until today, I have always preached that Biblical priorities followed four levels: 1) personal relationship with God, 2) family, 3) church/ministry, and 4) work. Granted it has always been impossible, as a pastor, to separate church and work, but my relationship with the Lord and family have been non-negotiable for nearly forty years.

One of the most sobering questions people ask me is, "What would you have done if Clark had died?" I've thought about that a lot since the accident. For the first two weeks, I really thought he would die and I started to feel the grief of him being gone from my life. To answer the question honestly, I would have to say I don't know. It didn't happen, so I can only speculate on what I would have done. I vividly remember one church member saying he was surprised I could even stay in the ministry after what we had gone through. I guess he must have thought I was blaming God.

I don't know what I would have done or how I would have felt, but I do know I would not have been filled with regret over not spending time with my son. I'm not saying in a prideful way that I have always been the best father. I've failed in many ways to live up to the ideals I set for myself and, for sure, to the principles about parenting in the Bible. But when it comes to spending time with your child and being involved in his life, I think I finally got something right.

The best way I can explain it is that he and I have always been best friends. I was there to cut the umbilical cord when he was born and I've been in his face ever since. When he was an infant and I was in seminary, Debbie and I would reverse our work schedules so we wouldn't have to put him in daycare. It meant a lot of evening and night shifts for her and a lot of meetings and visits with a pumpkin seat in tow for me, but it worked for our family.

Unless I was out of town, I never missed a school function, or a ballgame, or a doctor's visit. I coached many of his sports teams and loved spending hours on the sidelines just watching him practice. What about the times there were deacon's meetings or Sunday school class socials on ballgame nights? The deacons met without me and everyone in the class ate what I wasn't there to consume. They lived and I had a life with my son. It's a choice I made long before Clark was ever born. So much of what we allow to take away time with our families isn't really as important as we think it is. If you would be honest with others and let them know how important your family time is to you, they would probably encourage you rather than oppose you.

In spite of the obstacles, Debbie and I always tried to focus on being together with Clark. There were trips to Disneyworld and the beach. We would take him to play putt-putt, or laser tag, or ride his bike in the parking lot. Clark received a craft box every month which he and his Momma would put together. She would tickle him until he squealed and I would play video games with him until he nearly fell asleep. Best of all we would talk and talk and talk. We'd talk about school and about his friends. Later on we'd talk about girls, broken hearts and most importantly, faith. There was no subject that was off limits. If it interested him then it interested us. We did anything and everything we could think of to make memories together.

Memories are important things to leave behind to the people you love. In those memories are important values and lessons about our faith. For now, until I get to Heaven and can see him again, the memories of my Dad are all I have. But they have the power to guide me even now. When I have a critical decision to make, I often think of what my Dad would have done. His character rubs off on me through those memories. The time he decided to spend with me can never be taken away from me and contributes to the man I am today. I thank God for the gift of memories.

I mentioned in a previous chapter about how much influence music has had on my life. I recently heard the song *One Life To Love* by the group 33 Miles. It's a song about how to live your life with few regrets. The chorus says, *"You only get just one time around. You only get one shot at this. One chance to find out the one thing that you don't want to miss. One day when it's all said and done, I hope you see that it was enough. This one ride, one try, one life to love."*

Truer words were never spoken. We don't get a "do over" with our lives, so the only way to get it right is to get it right now. We may not be able to go back and undo the past, but from this point forward we can commit ourselves to getting our priorities in line with God's priorities. The first thing God did after he created the universe was to create the first family. He didn't create an organization to worship him but instead he created a home where his love and character could be lived out on a daily basis.

If May 7th, 2005 had been the last day of my son's life here on earth, it would have broken my heart and crushed my spirit. But it would not have filled my heart with regrets.

# Shark Bites

*"So do not give me any more trouble. I have scars on my body
that show I belong to Christ Jesus."*
Galatians 6:17 (NCV)

When Clark was five years old, we took him on a family trip
to Universal Studios in Orlando. We had a great time together
– well, except for one day. That was the day we decided to take
him on the Jaws ride. It seemed like a timid enough ride to go
on. It mainly consisted of several boats that circled slowly around
a lagoon. There weren't any big drops or fast corners, so it looked
safe for a kindergartner.

As we settled into our row of seats on the boat, we decided
to put Clark on the inside so he could see more of the lagoon
we were going to circle. That was a bad idea. When the ride was
nearing the end, a life-like mechanical Jaws rose up out of the
water, with an open mouth and lunged towards the boat. You
guessed it. It lunged right at Clark. It scared him so badly that
he wouldn't get in the bathtub for days. Still today he can't stand
the "duh, duh" sound of the Jaws theme song. It probably scarred
him for life!

Scars are just that way. They stay with us for a lifetime as a
result of something that happened to us. We probably all have a
few. I have several from my sports injuries to remind me I used

to be an athlete. Clark has several as a result of the car wreck. He has several on the back of his right hand from the broken glass and metal. He has a few on the back of his head as a result of not being able to be moved in the PICU. He blends in fine in Kentucky because when he cuts his hair short, they look like a perfect cat's paw. People think he intentionally got it cut that way because he's a U.K. fan.

Then there are a series of craters down the outside of his left leg. There are six of them and they start near the hip and extend to the knee. I was shocked when one day he said, "Dad, when I go to the beach and a hot chick asks me what happened to my leg, I think I'm just going to tell her it was a shark bite. That will be easier and more impressive". You've got to be kidding me!

One day Debbie was noticing Clark's scars and started to get teary-eyed. When we asked her what was the matter, she told us it made her sad to see his scars and that she wished there was a way to get rid of them. Clark looked at her and said, "I don't ever want them to go away. Every time I look at them they remind me that God saved my life."

What about you? How long has it been since you've done an inventory on all your scars? Scars you've received from relationships. Scars that are yours because someone let you down. Scars from mistakes you've made. Scars that are with you due to the abuse or violence of others. We all have lots of scars.

If Clark had said that looking at his scars bothered him, then we probably would have visited a plastic surgeon and explored options to have them removed. But what good would it have really done? Fixing the scar doesn't change the event which caused the scar, does it? Nothing will ever remove May 7th, 2005 from his history. Nothing will ever erase what happened in your life either.

If you stop and think about it, a scar has one positive thing about it. It is a sign healing has occurred. The scar covers over the place that was once wounded and is now healed. The scar itself may cause some minor pain or discomfort but it's never as bad as the original injury.

Have you experienced healing for the things that have caused deep wounds in your life? If not, they will only continue to keep you trapped in pain and fear. Healing needs to take place before the wounds begin to threaten your very life. But where do you start?

I believe the first step is always to acknowledge what has happened. So many times we try to hide the hurts or rationalize away the pain and it gets us nowhere. Maybe the place for you to start is to admit you have a wound that needs to be healed. A second step may be to seek out help. There are a lot of us, especially we guys, who shrug off our injuries and say we'll be alright. Well, how's that working out for you now? Maybe we need a friend, a trusted counselor or pastor to help us deal with the emotional baggage we've been carrying around so long.

In the end, however, there is only one source for healing and that's the Lord. One of our favorite doctors, Clark's orthopedic surgeon used to say, "God does the healing. I just collect the fee!" He's exactly right. God can do what needs to be done in your life for real healing to begin. He invites you to come to him with all your hurts and burdens. Jesus said, *"Come to me, all of you who are weary and carry heavy burdens, and I will give you rest."* - Matthew 11:28 (NLT) He's always available to listen to us and ready to act on our behalf.

Some of our wounds come from decisions we've made that we wish we could go back and change. We need the kind of forgiveness only God can give to us. Some of our wounds come from the hurts others have caused us. Jesus certainly knows what it feels like to be hurt and betrayed by others and yet be able to say from the Cross, "Father, forgive them, for they do not know what they do." (Luke 23:34, NKJV)

Jesus is no stranger to wounds. His death was pictured for us by the prophet Isaiah when he said the Savior was "wounded for the wrong we did; he was crushed for the evil we did. The punishment, which made us well, was given to him, and we are healed because of his wounds." (Isaiah 53:5, NCV)

Jesus died a real death on the cross in order to provide the basis for God's forgiveness for us. His hands and his feet were wounded as they drove the nails through them and into the cross that day. He gave his life so you and I could experience a new life by trusting him completely with our sins and with our lives.

It may take a while but your wounds will heal. The healing will leave behind scars to remind you of that healing. Take a minute right now to look proudly upon your scars and remember what God has brought you through. When you look at them, don't focus on the pain which cause them but upon the God who healed them and thank him for his faithfulness in your life.

Our family's prayer for you, as you have been reading about God's miraculous healing in our lives, has been that you would open your heart to the One who can make all things new. He was our only hope and he is yours. His promise to us is that He will walk with us through the valley of the shadow of death so we don't have to live in fear anymore. He was our 4th man in the car that night and he is able to protect and keep us. Most importantly he has prepared a place for us in Heaven where we won't have to deal with our scars anymore.

# Clark Today

At the publishing of this book, Clark is now just past 6 years in his recovery and we continue to be amazed at the extent to which God has both healed and blessed him. Clark is on track to graduate from Western Kentucky University in December of 2011 with a Bachelor's Degree in Computer Information Technology. This will be only 18 months later than he would have been able to graduate if the accident had never occurred. We are so grateful to God for his blessings.

Even more exciting for our family is Clark's recent engagement to Marylee Colvin. They have set their wedding date for October 2012. We are so thankful to have Marylee as part of our family. Long before they met, she had already heard about Clark's story from mutual friends and had prayed for his recovery. She has been extremely supportive and understanding of the minor challenges that Clark still struggles with such as short term memory loss. She is, without a doubt, the woman we had always prayed that God would provide for our son.

In order to keep all of our friends and family up to date with Clark's story, we have established www.thefourthmaninthecar.com . We invite you to visit it often for a more complete picture of God's continuing miracle in Clark's life.

CPSIA information can be obtained at www.ICGtesting.com
Printed in the USA
LVOW070442291111

256826LV00001B/44/P